A Connecticut Christmas

DIANE SMITH

Guilford, Connecticut

Text copyright © 2011 by Diane Smith

Project editor: David Legere
Text design: Sheryl P. Kober
Layout: Melissa Evarts

Library of Congress Cataloging-in-Publication Data is available on file.

ISBN 978-0-7627-2669-1

Printed in China
10 9 8 7 6 5 4 3 2 1

It's Christmas in Connecticut, from the Berkshires to the Sound,
And along each winding river, in each and every town.

—TOM CALLINAN

CONTENTS

ACKNOWLEDGMENTS

"Yes, we can!" It's not just a campaign slogan. It's the motto that guides the life of my husband, Tom Woodruff. On the heels of finishing one book, it was immediately time to start this one. With only three months to research, report, write, shoot, and experience the fifty best things about a Connecticut Christmas, I wasn't sure it could be done. But Tom said, as he always does, "Yes, we can!" Tom, thank you for working all through the season when other people are relaxing and celebrating. Although we had little time to decorate a tree, shop for presents, or send out holiday cards, you realized that *A Connecticut Christmas* is a joy to be shared, and we did just that—at concerts and festivals, parades and nativity scenes.

"Yes, we can," said Erin Turner, the editor who lives in Montana but is now a Connecticut aficionado. To the team at Globe Pequot Press, thanks for your enthusiasm. To my collaborator, Lisa Franco, thanks for saying "Yes, we can" when it was time to seek out one more event or make one more phone call.

Thanks to all the organizations and friends who said, "Yes, we can find photos," which now enhance each story. Thanks, especially, to the talented photographers who captured the character of *A Connecticut Christmas*.

INTRODUCTION: FEELING FESTIVE

"Connecticut is *the* place to spend Christmas," says Bill Raymond, who stars each year as Ebenezer Scrooge in *A Christmas Carol* at the Hartford Stage. I agree with him. Connecticut was the first New England state to declare Christmas a legal holiday, in 1845. Two hundred Christmases in Connecticut had already passed.

Christmas is on my mind all year. I'm always on the lookout for unusual ornaments. As we decorate the tree, I love reminiscing with my husband, Tom, about the event that inspired the purchase of each one.

There's the lobster claw hand-painted with a majestic tall ship by a man in Niantic. We found the globes painted with images of Connecticut lighthouses at Mystic Seaport and the Maritime Aquarium in Norwalk. Christmas is about memories, family, and tradition. Decorating the tree each year is the touchstone that brings it all together.

What a wonderful musical score has been written over the ages to accompany Christmas! All over Connecticut, chorales, choirs, orchestras, chamber groups, and bands of every description fill the air with Christmas music, from the glory of Handel's *Messiah* at the Bushnell to the medieval merriment at Connecticut College's Make We Joy concert, to the avant-garde score of *Unsilent Night* performed on boom boxes in New Haven. There is music in Christmas for everyone. Even our pageants and parades include time for a community carol sing. It is truly the time of year to make a joyful noise!

"Deck the Halls" is one of the carols we sing, and from the extreme to the exquisite, decorating is an essential element of the holidays. To me, the classic Colonial home with a slender white candle in each window, a wreath on the door, and evergreen roping along a picket fence says Christmas in Connecticut.

assured me. "You don't think Dad and Mom could afford all these toys for five kids, do you?" That was pretty persuasive at the time. And I still believe in Santa Claus. I know he exists because I see him everywhere. He may not live at the North Pole, or look like the Santa you see at the mall, but he truly has Santa's spirit of generosity and love.

Sometimes the Santa who lives among us is an older gentleman, with white hair and rosy cheeks, like Eric Hultgren, the Toy Man. Eric delivered handmade wooden toys all year long to the sick children at Bridgeport Hospital. Eric is gone now, but I still think of him at this time of year.

Sometimes these real-life Santas are women, like Barbara Bellinger, who hosts an elegant holiday tea party in Bridgeport each year to raise money to help fight breast cancer. Sometimes Santa arrives not in a sleigh powered by eight tiny reindeer but in a helicopter, as Brian Tague does when recognizing the service of our coastline's lighthouse keepers and Coast Guard stations.

What motivates these real-life Santas? What infects them with a superabundance of holiday spirit? Sometimes giving to others is their way of overcoming loss, as it was for Eric, who started making toys while his wife was seriously ill. Sometimes they are moved by thankfulness, as in Barbara Bellinger's case. A breast cancer survivor, she is grateful to live to see another Christmas, her favorite time of year. Sometimes it's for the pure joy of seeing a

The settlers of our state didn't believe in festive celebrations of Christmas. The curator of the Stanley-Whitman House in Farmington will tell you that Christmas was just another day on the calendar—that is, until reformers like Harriet Beecher Stowe began sowing the seeds of the traditions we love today.

Some of our neighbors let their decorated homes tell of their joy, like Rita Giancola, who needs weeks to put up all of her holiday decorations in New Britain. Mike and Kathy Longhi spent thirty years turning their place in Torrington into a breathtaking display that covers most of an acre and includes a giant snowman, who is nineteen feet tall and covered in thirteen thousand lights.

As a little girl I once asked my dad, "Is there really a Santa Claus?" "Of course there is," he smile on the face of a child, as it is for the hundreds who turn out to wrap packages at St. Luke's Life-Works in Stamford.

So Santa may not be a jolly old elf in a fur-trimmed red suit. Santa may be the woman at work who organizes a giving tree, so that needy children will have gifts on Christmas morning. Santa may wear a Marine Corps uniform and collect thousands of toys to give away in the poorest parts of town. Santa may be the friend who calls you in the middle of the holiday rush and urges you to slow down, at least for an hour, and come to church for a Christmas concert and a chance to meditate on the real meaning of Christmas. During the Christmas season in Connecticut, you don't have to look far to find Santa; his spirit is all around you.

CONNECTICUT CHRISTMAS TREES

Legend has it that Hendrick Roddmore in Windsor Locks decorated the first Christmas tree in Connecticut in 1777, a tradition he brought from his German homeland. He must have had many trees to choose from, for Windsor Locks at the time was known as Pine Meadow, but the legend has never been proved or disproved. Some are convinced that Roddmore's tree really was the first Christmas tree in the New World; there are accounts, however, of Christmas trees in Pennsylvania German communities as early as 1747.

Regardless of when the tradition started in Connecticut, the tradition of Christmas trees stuck.

At **Maple Lane Farms,** in Preston, families come back year after year to cut their trees and often visit throughout the year, since Allyn Brown grows a cornucopia of pick-your-own fruits and veggies. Brown is also the biggest grower of black currants in North America.

In Shelton, harvesting your own tree at **Jones Family Farms** has been a tradition since the 1940s. Today more than one hundred thousand trees grow on the farm's two hundred hillside acres. With each harvest-your-own Christmas tree, a family receives a special dated and farm-designed pewter ornament from Woodbury Pewter. The farm offers freshly cut trees in the barnyard, as well as wreaths and garland. The Holiday Gatherings Gift Shop in a former dairy barn sells ornaments, farm-grown herbal products, and lots of craft items. Hot mulled cider and fresh-baked cookies are a must after cutting your tree, and a stop at the bonfire will warm you up.

And **Noden-Reed Park,** where Hendrick Roddmore is reputed to have decorated that first tree, is owned by the town of Windsor Locks and operated by the Windsor Locks Historical Society. The museum is open from May through October, but there is an open house at Christmastime, giving visitors a taste of the holidays of yesteryear and paying tribute to Hendrick Roddmore's pioneering Christmas tree.

MAPLE LANE FARMS
57 NW Corner Road, Preston, CT 06365
(860) 889-3766; www.maplelane.com

JONES FAMILY FARMS
606 Walnut Tree Hill Road, Shelton, CT 06484-2054
(203) 929-8425; www.jonesfamilyfarms.com

NODEN-REED PARK MUSEUM
58 West Street, Windsor Locks, CT 06096-1808
(860) 627-9212

O LITTLE TOWN

The Christmas spirit settles peacefully over Bethlehem, Connecticut—except at the post office, which is busier than Santa's North Pole workshop. In the first eleven months of the year, the post office handles about 250,000 pieces of mail. In the four weeks between Thanksgiving and Christmas, clerks process another 250,000 pieces—made up mostly of greeting cards from people who want their holiday cards postmarked Bethlehem, the Christmas Town.

In addition to the official postmark, customers love the cachets—rubber stamps with holiday designs—created by local artists, postal employees, and even schoolchildren. There's a new one every year going back to 1938, and the entire collection is available to stamp your cards.

Despite working seven days a week at this time of year, postal clerk Sally Cullen says, "It's great to see the people come in. They come year after year as a holiday tradition, and they spend the afternoon stamping their cards and having a really special holiday moment."

You might wonder if the rest of the year seems a little dull after the Christmas rush. "Yes," says one of the clerks with a smile, "but we need eleven months to rest up after this!"

A good time to visit and stamp your cards is during the annual Christmas Town Festival held the first Friday and Saturday in December, when the post office extends its hours. If you'd like to get in on the Christmas cheer but can't make your way to Bethlehem, the postmaster will help. Send your addressed, stamped cards in a parcel to the post office, addressed to the postmaster, and the clerks will postmark them for you and send them on, at no extra charge. Some years batches of cards have come in from more than half the United States and half a dozen foreign countries.

There is a feeling of Yuletide pride in this Litchfield County town, according to Maureen Vescera, who lives in Bethlehem. "It's the best small town in Connecticut. This is the true meaning of Christmas."

BETHLEHEM POST OFFICE
34 East Street, Bethlehem, CT 06751
(203) 266-7910; www.christmastownfestival.com

THE FLYING SANTA

In early December 1929, aviation pioneer William Wincapaw encountered a storm just off the Maine coast. He followed the beacons from the lighthouses and managed to fly home safely. To show his gratitude, Wincapaw made a return flight over the lighthouses on Christmas Day, dropping small gifts to the lighthouse keepers he believed had saved his life. The Flying Santa, a New England tradition, was born.

As time passed and nearly all the lighthouses were automated, the next Flying Santa, Edward Rowe Snow, decided that the Coast Guard personnel who maintained the lights and kept the waterways safe should be thanked, too, so he expanded Santa's route, including navigation and boat stations from New York to Maine. All the Santas since Snow have kept that spirit alive.

The Stratford Point Lighthouse is automated and operated by computers now, but U.S. Coast Guard Lieutenant Judson Coleman and his family live there. On a December afternoon the Colemans host staff from Coast Guard Station New Haven and their families for a visit from Flying Santa.

St. Nick (also known as Chief Warrant Officer Thomas Guthlein) lightly touches down in a helicopter flown and owned by civilian pilot Evan Wile.

Four-year-old Parker Phillips's eyes are wide as his mom, a Coast Guard lieutenant, explains that Santa doesn't always arrive in a sleigh.

Brian Tague, the president of Friends of Flying Santa, arranges the flights and raises money for all the expenses. He grins as the kids cluster around, clamoring for toys from Santa's pack. "This is a gesture of appreciation for their Coast Guard service, just to say thanks."

As Brian climbs back into the sleek black chopper and heads for his next stop, Santa waves and shouts to the kids, "Now don't you tell Rudolph about this helicopter!"

If you would like to make a contribution:

Friends of Flying Santa, Inc.
P.O. Box 80047, Stoneham, MA 02180-0001
(781) 438-4587; www.flyingsanta.com

SWEET MARIA'S

The morning of December 23, Maria Bruscino Sanchez is hand-painting poinsettias on sugar cookies the size of your palm. The rest of the staff, dressed in hot pink jackets and black-and-white-checked baker's caps, is rolling dough, sliding trays of cookies in and out of the oven, and packaging platters of goodies. They are preparing for Christmas Eve, the busiest day of the year at Sweet Maria's Bakery in Waterbury.

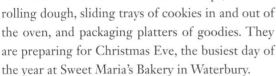

Baking has been part of Maria's life for as long as she can remember. Both her mother and grandmother baked, and aunts and great-aunts were generous with recipes and helpful hints.

"I don't know a lot of technical baking things, but several people on my staff do, because they went to culinary school; I learn a lot from them," she says. "I just do things the way people would do them in their home, only they don't have time."

Although Maria worked in a bakery in high school, she never intended to make cookies and cakes for a living. She put her marketing degree to work at an advertising firm for a few years, but recalls, "I always baked cakes out of my house for family and friends, and then it turned into a booming home business. My husband totally encouraged me to open a bakery."

It was a bold move for a young woman, but it paid off. Sweet Maria's has been in business for twenty years. There's a family atmosphere in the shop, where Maria works side by side with her husband, parents, and cousins. "Everybody else who works here feels like family because we spend so much time together," she says with a chuckle, as the team picks up the rhythm of what Maria calls the "prepping and schlepping" that comes before the actual baking.

Offered a platter of cookies, it's impossible to choose a favorite. Pignoli cookies and almond macaroons are the most popular, though it is hard to beat her sumptuous peanut-butter balls, Mexican wedding cookies, lemon drops, or biscotti. They're all so scrumptious you might say Maria Bruscino Sanchez wrote the book on cookies. You'd be right too. The title is *Sweet Maria's Italian Cookie Tray: A Cookbook*, filled with recipes for sweet treats.

Sweet Maria's Bakery
159 Manor Avenue, Waterbury, CT 06705
(203) 755-3804 or (888) 755-4099
www.sweet-marias.com
Some items are available by mail order.

CANDLELIGHT CAROLING AT LOURDES

Though most people who make the pilgrimage to Lourdes in Litchfield come when the leaves on the trees form a canopy over this church without walls, the shrine is open year-round. The annual Christmas Festival draws the faithful, despite wintry weather. Thirty thousand people flock here each year to pray at the stone grotto, which resembles the place in France where Catholics believe the Virgin Mary appeared to a young girl.

In 1958 two of the brothers from the Montfort community in Italy arrived and constructed the shrine. From May through mid-October, three resident priests celebrate Mass and anoint the sick here. During the winter months, Mass is said indoors, in the Grotto Chapel.

Some visitors walk alone, climbing a quarter-mile-long trail through the woods that leads them through the Way of the Cross, depicting the suffering and death of Christ in bronze figures.

People who visit say they feel a holy presence here, and never more so than at Christmas, when they gather to celebrate Christ's birth. Montfort House, located on the property, offers religious retreats for individuals and small groups.

Candlelight caroling is one of three highlights of the annual Christmas Festival Weekend at the shrine. On Saturday morning families work together to construct gingerbread nativity scenes. That evening the scent of pine trees wafts through the chilly night air as carolers, clutching candles, are led to the grotto by the glow of five hundred luminaria lining the walkway. On Sunday afternoon at 3:00 and 4:00 p.m., more than one hundred children from community churches stage a living nativity outside, complete with livestock. As visitors stroll the long walkway through the property, characters from the Christmas pageant share a spiritual message with them.

For those who visit in December, Lourdes of Litchfield is a peaceful place to meditate on the true meaning of Christmas.

Lourdes in Litchfield Shrine
50 Montfort Road, P.O. Box 667
Litchfield, CT 06759
(860) 567-1041; www.shrinect.org

HOLIDAY GLOW

A single candle in a window is a holiday tradition in New England, but this is the season of light, and Connecticut is all aglow.

At the **Festival of Silver Lights at Hubbard Park** in Meriden, the beauty of the heavily wooded park lends an air of wonder to hundreds of lighted displays. Emerging from a quiet wooded cove is a family of deer and a mama bear and her cubs. Walter Hubbard, who donated the land for the park in the 1890s, would have loved this. His company

produced electric light fixtures. Meriden's Parks and Recreation Department creates the display, with an emphasis on local culture. There's a lighted replica of Castle Craig, a Meriden landmark, and a field of daffodils, a reminder of the city's Daffodil Festival, a highlight of spring. Dolphins leap from Mirror Lake while camels trot over snow-covered fields. Lighted birds perch overhead. There are half a million lights twinkling over sixty-seven acres.

The **United Illuminating Fantasy of Lights** in New Haven helps light a flame of hope for people with disabilities. The show is a fund-raiser for Easter Seals Goodwill Industries, which helps people with disabilities live independently. The show is organized into themed sections. Turn on your radio for holiday music, and drive through Toyland, Candyland, and Winter Wonderland. Since the show is located at the most popular beach in New Haven, it capitalizes on summer fun, featuring a sailboat, a tugboat, and Santa on a Jet Ski. The city donates the park space, and local unions donate countless hours of labor to erect the displays. Each night a local company, organization, or family provides the volunteers to sell tickets.

The Hartford **Festival of Light** sets Constitution Plaza aglow with two hundred thousand white lights from the day after Thanksgiving until Three Kings Day in January. The lighting ceremony is the official kickoff for the holiday season in the capital city. Santa Claus is the guest of honor at the event, which features live music and a sing-along. The entire plaza is illuminated, along with a giant tree, a cascading waterfall in the fountain, and statues of angels and deer designed by the same artist whose sculptures adorn Rockefeller Center in New York City.

FESTIVAL OF SILVER LIGHTS AT HUBBARD PARK
West Main Street
Meriden, CT 06450
(203) 630-4259 or (203) 630-4260
www.cityofmeriden.org

UNITED ILLUMINATING FANTASY OF LIGHTS
Lighthouse Point Park
2 Lighthouse Road
New Haven, CT 06512-4311
Easter Seals Phone: (203) 777-2000
www.newhavengoodwill.easterseals.com

FESTIVAL OF LIGHT
Constitution Plaza
Hartford, CT 06103
Greater Hartford Arts Council
(860) 525-8629; www.LetsGoArts.org

CHRISTMAS TROUBADOUR

Tom Callinan has not only been to most of the 169 towns in Connecticut, but he's also written songs about many of them. At last count he had penned well over a hundred Connecticut songs—more than anyone else. So Tom knows a thing or two about Christmas in Connecticut.

Some folks go to Bethlehem to stamp their
Christmas cards,
And others visit Mystic, with its spars and masts
and yards.
Where jolly old St. Nicholas rides the Essex train,
And fifes and drums by torchlight march down Old
Saybrook's Main.

As he wrote in the lyrics to another song, like the Christmas tree he cuts each year, he is "Connecticut grown."

So Tom sings about everything from Connecticut farms to Connecticut highways, which helps explain why he was named Connecticut's first State Troubadour after a hearing in the state legislature, where a lawmaker asked if he had ever written a song about Interstate 91.

"I said no, but I am working on a song about I-95. He said, 'If you wrote about 91, you'd have a better chance of getting this bill out of committee,'" Tom says, grinning. "So I quickly went home and erased the 5 and put in a 1 and wrote 'Connecticut's Lifeline I-91': *'Connecticut's lifeline is I-91, a lesson in patience where the work's never done,'*" he sings.

For a man who can wax poetic about a traffic jam, dashing off a ditty about Connecticut's fall foliage should have been a breeze. Not so. He told me that this one caused writer's block. "It took me over three years to write that song because there is no rhyme for the word *orange* in the English language," he said with a chuckle.

Eventually he worked it out. The song "Christmas in Connecticut" came easy, though:

Towns and cities, large and small, light their
Christmas trees,
And the hearty souls brave wind and cold for
living nativities,
At sites throughout the Nutmeg State, dazzling
displays
Await the throngs that venture out right up
through Three Kings Day.

CRACKERBARREL ENTERTAINMENTS
55 East Town Street
Norwich, CT 06360
Phone/Fax: (860) 889-6648
www.crackerbarrel-ents.com/Callinan/bio.htm

HANDMADE HOLIDAYS

If you're on the trail of handmade gifts, five non-profit crafts education centers in Connecticut are the places to shop. Proceeds from holiday sales support the artists and the centers.

The **Guilford Art Center** nurtures students who study everything from blacksmithing to photography. The holiday sale, titled "Artistry," highlights the work of 350 artists from across the country.

In Middletown you'll find more than just pottery at **Wesleyan Potters,** where a cooperative guild of artists also turns out metal, clay, and fiber.

The **Farmington Valley Arts Center** is located in refurbished brownstone buildings once occupied by a safety fuse manufacturer and now offers studios to more than forty artists.

The **Brookfield Craft Center** just north of Danbury is located in six vintage buildings along the Still River, which include studios, galleries, and living space for visiting faculty. The holiday sale is spread over three floors in a gristmill that dates to 1780 and overlooks Halfway Falls.

In New Haven's Audubon Arts District the **Creative Arts Workshop** sells the work of more than three hundred artists in a seven-week event that attracts over ten thousand visitors.

GUILFORD ART CENTER
411 Church Street, Guilford, CT 06437
(203) 453-5947; www.guilfordartcenter.org

WESLEYAN POTTERS
350 South Main Street
Middletown, CT 06457-4213
(860) 344-0039; www.wesleyanpotters.com

FARMINGTON VALLEY ARTS CENTER
25 Arts Center Lane, Avon Park North
Avon, CT 06001
(860) 678-1867; www.artsfvac.org/

BROOKFIELD CRAFT CENTER
286 Whisconier Road, Brookfield, CT 06804
(203) 775-4526; www.brookfieldcraftcenter.org

CREATIVE ARTS WORKSHOP
80 Audubon Street, New Haven, CT 06510
(203) 562-4927; www.creativeartsworkshop.org

Milk Chocolate
Santa (5.25oz) -$6.99
Santa (3oz) -$3.99
Snowman (3oz) -$3.99

THE CHOCOLATE FACTORY

Christmas comes early at the **Thompson Candy Company** in Meriden. By midsummer Santa Claus has come to town at the chocolate factory that opened its doors in 1879.

Not just one Santa but thousands and thousands of chocolate Santas march along a conveyor belt, from molding to wrapping. Forty-two million mini chocolate ornaments and a couple of million bells and other chocolate treats will be shipped around the world, according to Jeff White, the owner and president of Thompson Candy Company. The chocolate they use is made according to Jeff's secret recipe.

Thompson candy is coveted not only for its taste but also for old-fashioned decorative touches like hand-tied bows on the wrappings. That care has been handed down through three generations of Thompsons and two generations of Whites. Some employees have worked here for decades, since the days when Jeff's dad owned the business. One reason might be the perks. "We allow the employees to eat all they want," Jeff says with a smile, and admits that he is a bit of a chocoholic. He even met his wife while she was working behind a candy counter.

If you're strolling along the green in Guilford, stop in at the **Village Chocolatier.** Ingrid Collins's shop isn't much bigger than a shoebox, but it is crammed with the finest chocolate from all over, including French truffles, gourmet malted milk balls, and extra dark chocolate nonpareils. In spite of the store's diminutive size, Ingrid says she is the biggest seller of Thompson candy in the state, and she and her staff find ways to turn the foil-covered candies into special holiday gifts, packaged with an ornament or a Christmas bell.

At the Village Chocolatier in Guilford and at Thompson Candy Company in Meriden, the holidays are extra sweet.

THOMPSON CANDY is sold in stores nationwide.

Factory outlet store:
80 South Vine Street, Meriden, CT 06451
(203) 235-2541; www.thompsoncandy.com

VILLAGE CHOCOLATIER
79 Whitfield Street, Guilford, CT 06437-2631
(203) 453-5226

TREES OF HOPE

Remember the way you felt as a child, looking at your Christmas tree? It seemed a magical thing, all glitter and sparkle, garland and twinkle. You'll feel that way again when you see the magic made by the decorators at the annual Fairfield Christmas Tree Festival.

Three hundred volunteers transform the Burr Homestead, a stately Greek Revival home, into a glitzy winter showplace. Thirty decorators and designers create dozens of lavishly decorated trees, wreaths, and doorway swags to fill the nineteen spaces; every room and hallway is done up, and even the staircases are adorned. An upstairs room is transformed into a winter fantasy its creators call "First Snow on the Birch Forest," sparkling with aqua, silver, snow, and fairy dust. Each year the designs are different, but they always include lavish table settings and rooms themed for kids. Every item is for sale, and volunteers from local garden clubs will make custom wreaths for your door while you shop in the gift boutique.

The festival started nearly thirty years ago and has raised more than $2 million for nonprofits, including a local cancer center and Operation Hope, which helps the hungry and homeless.

Kristin Nick, the Fairfield Christmas Tree Festival board president, says, "It's a lot of late nights and stressful moments working up to it, but I will say that the overall feeling shared by everyone working together is that we are really doing something amazing for our community."

The Burr Homestead is one of the most historic homes in Fairfield County. Peter Burr built the original house on the site in 1700. John Hancock and Dorothy Quincy were married there in 1775. Many notables visited, including George Washington, Benjamin Franklin, and John Adams. Aaron Burr, a cousin, was a frequent guest.

The Fairfield Christmas Tree Festival is kicked off by a gala preview party on the first Thursday evening after Thanksgiving. During the three-day fund-raiser there are five events, including a house tour, a children's activity, a tea, and a movie matinee.

THE BURR HOMESTEAD
739 Old Post Road
Fairfield, CT 06824
www.fairfieldchristmastreefestival.org

"These are the only authentic Christmas tree ornaments," says Hank Paine, owner of The Connecticut Store in Waterbury, as he hands me an intricately carved wooden disc. It's one of Paine's favorite puns, and this one may be true, because the ornaments made by Ken Killer are crafted from the trunks of actual Christmas trees.

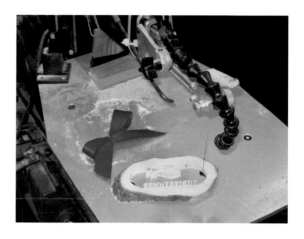

"When I retired, I said, 'I gotta do something'—I hate sitting around." Ken, a former high school biology teacher, explains: "We started making wooden toys. My wife and I both love toys, and we collect them, so I started making replicas of 1920 Mack trucks and sold some through Hank."

One day over coffee, Hank told Ken about the Paine family's tradition of saving a disc cut from the bottom of their tree, dating it, and hanging it on next year's tree, giving each tree a link to Christmases past. That gave Ken an idea. "I said, 'Bring me a blank and let's see if I can do something,' because I had just gotten a new scroll saw. So I scrolled out a date. It was about as simple a scrolling as you can do. I brought it back and he said, 'What else can you do?' I said, 'I don't know yet, but I bet we can do a lot.'"

Each year right after Christmas, Ken recycles about a hundred discarded trees for next season's ornaments. Ken has turned out about twelve thousand ornaments in the last few years, in about two hundred different designs that include everything from tropical fish to snowflakes. Maybe his designs have a little bit of magic. After all, his scroll saw is called Excalibur.

For these and other holiday gifts made in Connecticut, head for The Connecticut Store, online or in Waterbury.

THE CONNECTICUT STORE
116 Bank Street, Waterbury, CT 06702
(800) 474-6728; Fax: (203) 753-4128
www.theconnecticutstore.com

HARTFORD'S HERITAGE FROM SWEDEN

In Sweden the Christmas season begins on December 13, said to be the darkest day of the year. It is the day that Swedes celebrate as Santa Lucia Day. At dawn the eldest daughter in the family—dressed in a white robe with a red sash, and crowned with a wreath adorned with lit candles—awakens the household. The "Lucia Maiden" carries steaming coffee and *lussekatter* (saffron-flavored buns) to her family for breakfast.

The original Lucia is said to have lived in Sicily, where the young bride gave her entire dowry to the poor and admitted that she was a Christian. She was burned at the stake on December 13 in the year 304. She was later canonized by the Church, and anointed as Santa Lucia. A festival in her honor has been celebrated since the Middle Ages.

Swedes believe that during a period of famine in Värmland, an area of central Sweden, the saint was seen carrying food to the hungry, and so they have a special devotion to Lucia.

The Santa Lucia custom is an important part of the Christmas season at Emanuel Lutheran Church in Hartford, which was organized by Swedish immigrants more than a hundred years ago. Since 1914 the children of Emanuel have presented a Santa Lucia pageant, usually held on the first Friday evening in December.

The cast, which sings the entire program in Swedish, includes traditional characters like the Star Boy, Lantern Boy, and Baker Boys. The youngest members are only three years old and dressed as Tomtar, elves or household gnomes. Folklore says the Jul Tomtar watch over the home but can be mischievous if they don't get their bowls of rice pudding on Christmas Eve.

According to church member Terri Bienkowski, it is a special honor for the high school senior chosen each year to play Lucia. "We think of Lucia's light as the light of Christ, representing the warmth of the Christmas season," she says.

Although the Emanuel congregation is now made up of people of many nations, they still share the season with us in the Swedish way, with the Santa Lucia pageant followed by a reception featuring coffee, punch, and *pepparkakor*, thin, crunchy ginger snaps said to encourage a happy disposition.

EMANUEL LUTHERAN CHURCH
311 Capitol Avenue, Hartford, CT 06106-1495
(860) 525-0894; www.emanuelhartford.org

OLD SAYBROOK STROLL

One of the most sociable shopping events of the holiday season is the annual stroll in the charming shoreline town of Old Saybrook. Whether it's 60 degrees or freezing outside, crowds come out to enjoy activities ranging from a wreath sale to a spaghetti supper to horse-drawn hay rides on Main Street. Nearly every merchant offers refreshments, and many showcase entertainers. At Sound Runner, Dave Tiezzi is playing a sea chantey with his band, Save the Train, while kids and a few adults dance to the music.

Without a doubt, the star of the stroll for a decade was Siggy. The singing and keyboard-playing dachshund hung up his Santa suit in 2000, but for ten years he packed them in at the Paint Shop, giving performances every half-hour.

These days you're more likely to come across the Old Saybrook High School jazz ensemble swinging along with a packed house at the Paperback Cafe to the tunes of Duke Ellington and Buddy Rich. As the aromas of coffee and butternut bisque fill the air, band director Jeremy Taylor says, "Old Saybrook is a town where people love the arts."

That commitment to the arts is most evident in the newly opened Katharine Hepburn Cultural Arts Center, named in honor of the town's most prominent resident. The stroll commences with caroling on the balcony and a solemn moment when the Heroes Tree is lit in the lobby window by Gold Star Mothers including Kathryn Cross, who lost her son Tyler, a Navy SEAL. The tree is adorned with stars for the deceased, the injured, and others from Connecticut who are serving in the military.

The stroll is a night for families and kids, whether they are munching free kettle corn, caroling, or raising money for community projects. Dave DeMay is a soccer dad selling beautiful Woodbury Pewter ornaments for your tree. Each one commemorates a local landmark, like the Old Saybrook Outer Lighthouse, and raises funds for a college scholarship for a senior soccer player, chosen by the fans. The Old Saybrook Stroll is a great way to stoke your seasonal spirit, and start your shopping.

The stroll is held on Main Street in Old Saybrook the first Friday night in December.

ATHENEUM FESTIVAL OF TREES AND TRADITIONS

The nation's oldest public art museum, the Wadsworth Atheneum Museum of Art in Hartford is the breathtaking backdrop for the annual Festival of Trees and Traditions. Morgan Great Hall, with its two-story-high vaulted ceiling and crimson walls lined with art masterpieces, is one of the settings for lavishly adorned trees, centerpieces, garlands, and holiday decorations, all available for sale. They are created and donated by local artists, organizations, and individuals. Each tree is themed, and they range from splendid to silly to sweet. A tree called "Dreams, Hopes, and Wishes," designed by the Connecticut Association of Foster and Adoptive Parents, includes this message from Tyler: "I dream about being a baseball player. I wish for someone to make me a nice lunch every day. I hope that someday I will be adopted." Another, named "SEA-sons Greetings," is a splashy blue-and-white glitter tree nearly afloat with boats and tropical fish ornaments.

From late morning until late afternoon there is live entertainment, including musical performances by civic and school groups ranging from madrigal singers to a saxophone quartet. Storytelling and crafts workshops for kids are offered in Candy Lane.

The weeklong festival celebrates Christmas, Hanukkah, Kwanzaa, Three Kings Day, and the winter solstice. Kids can paint a kinara for Kwanzaa, play dreidel games for Hanukkah, or add their own Christmas wishes to the children's tree. A boutique sells ornaments, books, and gifts. Organized by the Women's Committee of the Wadsworth Atheneum, the Festival of Trees and Traditions is the largest public fund-raiser for the museum and involves nearly three hundred volunteers. The proceeds help underwrite everything from children's art supplies and the conservation of paintings to a documentary film series, lectures, and other special events.

Plan some extra time to browse through the museum's impressive collection of European art, including major works by Caravaggio, Degas, Cézanne, Renoir, Monet, Manet, and van Gogh. The American Painting and Sculpture collection encompasses Colonial-era portraits and history paintings, Hudson River School landscapes, post–Civil War era favorites, and examples of twentieth-century movements including Ash Can, Modernism, and Surrealism.

ATHENEUM FESTIVAL OF TREES AND TRADITIONS
Wadsworth Atheneum
600 Main Street, Hartford, CT 06103
(860) 278-2670; www.wadsworthatheneum.org

A VERY BARNUM CHRISTMAS

"As the celebration of the Christmas holiday was a fairly new concept to mid-nineteenth-century Americans, P. T. Barnum never included accounts of family festivities in his writings," says Kathy Maher, executive director and curator of Bridgeport's Barnum Museum. "He does mention, however, that Jenny Lind, the Swedish Nightingale, prepared a small traditional Christmas tree for her company during the acclaimed 1850 American tour, and her Swedish entourage enjoyed the lovely decorations and treats that were gathered for the holiday celebration."

Soprano Jenny Lind's tour of America was one of P. T. Barnum's boldest ventures. But "The Great American Showman," who most people associate with over-the-top entertainment like the circus, was also a visionary about his city and his country, and a man who proved himself by holding office as mayor of Bridgeport and a state legislator for Connecticut.

"Baby Bridgeport," the preserved elephant, greets visitors when they arrive at the museum's "Celebrate the Season" exhibit. He was born at the circus's winter quarters in Bridgeport, the second elephant born in captivity.

"The decorations in the museum's period rooms demonstrate how the ideal of Christmas became woven into an American tradition," says Kathy, who offers several interesting lectures during the holiday season that trace the evolution of Christmas customs from 1850 through 1900. The galleries are filled with festive decorations and costumes from the museum's collection.

Stroll through the rest of the three-story museum and enjoy artifacts like a reproduction of Barnum's renowned "humbug," the Fejee Mermaid, and a souvenir piece of cake from Tom Thumb's 1863 wedding. You'll learn about his life, including his humble beginnings in Bethel, Connecticut; the "curiosities and marvels of nature" in his American Museum on Broadway in New York City; his political life in Bridgeport, his adopted home; and his most-famous enterprise, "P. T. Barnum's Greatest Show On Earth."

Other activities include a gingerbread contest for kids, and workshops in which they can create Victorian tree ornaments and holiday cards. Preschoolers will enjoy the annual reading by the mayor or first lady of *The Night Before Christmas*.

THE BARNUM MUSEUM
820 Main Street, Bridgeport, CT 06604
(203) 331-1104; www.barnum-museum.org

CHRISTMAS IMPRESSIONS

Florence Griswold was born on Christmas Day in 1850. The daughter of a sea captain, Miss Florence, as she came to be known, grew up in one of the finest homes in Old Lyme. Years later, she opened her home as a boardinghouse for American impressionists, and they turned it into an artistic masterpiece.

"They very much loved the landscape and the sense of place that this corner of Connecticut has, with all of its low-lying river areas," says Jeffrey Andersen, director of the Florence Griswold Museum.

Artists like Childe Hassam, Willard Metcalf, and William Chadwick had great affection for the woman who opened her home and her heart to them. In tribute to her, they left behind works of art on her paneled walls, mantelpieces, and wooden doors.

In keeping with that tradition, a highlight of Christmas at the museum is "Miss Florence's Artist Tree," which stands twelve feet tall and is decorated with palettes painted and donated by more than a hundred artists from across the nation. Elaborate fantasy trees inspired by special exhibitions of paintings grace the Kriebel Gallery.

Christmas in the main house is extra special since it is also Miss Florence's birthday, and it is decorated for a 1910 Art Colony Christmas. A recent celebration featured a series of historic vignettes re-creating the bohemian spirit of the Old Lyme art colony. In the parlor a mannequin portrayed Miss Florence celebrating her birthday by receiving guests. The dining room, famous for its many panels painted by the artists, was set for a holiday feast.

There are special events throughout the season, ranging from a Teddy Bear Tea to hands-on holiday craft workshops. The museum shop is a place to find special gifts, including lavish art books and one-of-a-kind jewelry pieces.

The Florence Griswold Museum is worth a visit any time of year, but especially at Christmas, when the house is lovingly decorated and the spirit of Florence Griswold abounds.

FLORENCE GRISWOLD MUSEUM
96 Lyme Street, Old Lyme, CT 06371
(860) 434-5542; www.florencegriswoldmuseum.org

TREES IN THE RIGGING

Forget Santa's sleigh and eight tiny reindeer. In the river town of Essex, the jolly old elf arrives by boat. And in a town known for its history of shipbuilding, yachting, and steamboat traffic, why not? The annual event known as Trees in the Rigging starts with a late-afternoon parade, which begins at the town hall.

Along the way, historic characters from Essex Christmases past, including Lieutenant William Pratt, a well-known seventeenth-century ship owner, join the parade as it travels past antique homes done up with candles in windows and wreaths and evergreen garlands. It all ends up at the Steamboat Dock, where Santa arrives on one of many vessels of all shapes and sizes, with riggings dressed in holiday lights and colorful nautical flags.

Viewing the boat parade is best on the lawn of the **Connecticut River Museum,** at the foot of Main Street. The museum celebrates the cultural and natural heritage of the Connecticut River, and features a holiday exhibit that reflects the maritime history of Essex. Five hundred sailing vessels were built in Essex, including the *Oliver Cromwell*, Connecticut's first battleship, which was launched in 1775.

Other towns have recently launched holiday boat parades of their own.

The **Stamford Harbor Parade of Lights** attracts decorated boats that rendezvous at Czescik Municipal Marina and parade to the Crab Shell Restaurant at Stamford Landing. Awards are given for Most Creative, Most Original, Most Outrageous, and Best Decorated.

If you keep your boat commissioned into early winter, there's another Lighted Holiday Boat Parade in Mystic at the end of November. Vessels parade down the **Mystic River** and end up at **Mystic River Park.**

CONNECTICUT RIVER MUSEUM
67 Main Street, Essex, CT 06426
(860) 767-8269; www.ctrivermuseum.org

STAMFORD HARBOR PARADE OF LIGHTS
www.harborparade.com

MYSTIC RIVER AND MYSTIC RIVER PARK
Greater Mystic Chamber of Commerce
14 Holmes Street, P.O. Box 143, Mystic, CT 06355
(860) 572-9578; www.mysticchamber.org

A GRAND VICTORIAN HOLIDAY

LeGrand Lockwood would have enjoyed the holiday display of cast-iron toy trains in his former Norwalk home. The banker and railroad baron was able to see his own full-sized trains from the windows of his sixty-two-room home, the Gilded Age "cottage" now known as the Lockwood-Mathews Mansion Museum. Lockwood was a Norwalk native and its first millionaire. After Lockwood's untimely death, the property was sold to Charles Mathews, who lived there with his wife until 1938. The museum's annual Victorian holiday exhibition gives a pretty good idea of how the holidays were celebrated in the Victorian era when Christmas trees first became popular, after *Godey's Lady's Book* published a picture of Queen Victoria and Prince Albert's tree in 1846. The small, tabletop tree was decorated with nuts, dried fruits, and cookies. The trees became more elaborate in each succeeding decade. Candles were wired to the branches and small gifts tied on with ribbons. The candles were lighted for only a few minutes, and a bucket of water was kept nearby to douse any flare-ups.

From the 1870s through the turn of the twentieth century, ornaments became more elaborate. Fancy paper cutouts were sold to be trimmed with tinsel and turned into tree decorations. Ornaments of glass and tin were manufactured.

In the 1880s the earliest artificial trees were introduced to the United States from Germany. Goose feathers dyed green were attached to branches to resemble German white pines. Glass ornaments became popular and trees grew taller, some nearly touching the ceiling. President Grover Cleveland first tried out electric lights for trees in 1895.

1860s

1890s

One Victorian holiday tradition did not survive. A lady's magazine published a pattern for a costume designed to be worn by a child. It was the ultimate holiday adornment: a living, breathing Christmas tree!

The holiday season at LMMM includes lectures, parties, exhibits, and an enchanting candlelight tour.

Lockwood-Mathews Mansion Museum
295 West Avenue
Norwalk, CT 06850
(203) 838-9799
www.lockwoodmathewsmansion.com

CHRISTMAS VILLAGE

I'm just trying to do something good for Torrington because Torrington has always been so darned good to me." That's what Carl Bozenski said when he opened Christmas Village at Alvord Playground more than sixty years ago.

Carl was the city's first supervisor of parks and recreation, and he made sure that wintertime meant sledding and ice-skating for the local kids. But it was while Carl was far from his hometown that he came up with an idea that would become his living legacy. Carl was recovering from tuberculosis in a sanatorium in Norwich when he decided to invite Santa to spend part of December in Torrington. Carl figured Santa needed a nice place to stay and entertain his guests, so he built a one-room Tudor house for Santa's Throne Room; another little house is Santa's workshop. Santa's reindeer reside in a stable in the back.

Santa's helpers spend weeks preparing for his visit, stacking Santa's workshop from top to bottom with toys, rewiring the ones that use batteries, and then hiding control wires in a secret panel. One elf stands by when the kids stream into the room so he can make the toys come to life. Gus Lucia spent more than ten years working at the village, inspired by his own childhood visits there. "Being as little as I was, I thought it was a big, magical village," he says.

Each year the hottest doll of the season is added to the display. Favorite playthings made since 1947 populate the workshop. Santa's Throne Room is decked out with more decorations than you can count and yards of garland. Each child sits on Santa's knee and receives a gift to take home.

Many of the parents standing in line came to Santa's Throne Room when they were kids, including Lori Binstadt, who grew up in Litchfield. "It makes Christmas really special for the kids, and for me," she says.

That would have made Carl Bozenski very happy. After Carl died in 1986, the village was officially christened Carl Bozenski's Christmas Village.

CHRISTMAS VILLAGE
150 Church Street, Torrington, CT 06790
(860) 489-2274

BOUGHS OF HOLLY

For eighty-five years **Gilbertie's Herb Gardens** has been a family business, so stop in at their Westport store at Christmastime, and you are likely to run into Sal Gilbertie, or another member of the family, like his daughter-in-law, Carrie Gilbertie. Carrie was hosting an open house in their country store and greenhouse, which was stocked with herbal topiaries of sweet myrtle, rosemary, columnar basil, and lavender, as well as a host of poinsettias and amaryllis. Most of the growing is done at Gilbertie's Herb Farm in Easton, where twenty-three acres are planted with yarrow, sweet Annie, artemisia, sages, mints, anise hyssop, lamb's ear, and many other herbs. Over two hundred thousand square feet of greenhouses give the winter seedlings a good start. Gilbertie's is the largest herb plant grower in the country, and Sal has written several books over the years, teaching us how to use herbs in everything from cooking to holiday decorating.

Inventor Eli Whitney was the original owner of the twenty-plus acres that now comprise Edgerton Park in New Haven. In 1906 Frederick Brewster bought the property and called his estate "Edgerton," for its location on the edge of town. In accordance with Brewster's will, the large Tudor home was destroyed after his wife's death and the land was turned over to the city for a park. The park is listed on the National Register of Historic Places, and parts of the estate are still in use, including the greenhouses, which date to Brewster's time. The Edgerton Park Conservancy restored and maintains them, and has opened sections for community use. One wing is devoted to **Greenbrier Greenhouse,** where people with disabilities work and learn horticultural skills. Want to make someone smile from ear to ear? Stop by to purchase the poinsettias they've grown, or the wreaths they've made at Greenbrier. Retail sales help fund the supported employment program.

GILBERTIE'S HERB GARDENS
7 Sylvan Lane, Westport, CT 06880-4694
(203) 227-4175; www.gilbertiesherbs.com

GREENBRIER GREENHOUSE
75 Cliff Street, New Haven, CT 06511
(203) 777-1886

MAKE WE JOY

"'In the bleak midwinter,' as Christina Rossetti's poem reads, people have gathered for centuries at the winter solstice, Earth's darkest hour, to celebrate life and its renewal."

This is the message of the medieval merriment of Make We Joy, a raucous revelry based on the Old English tradition and celebrated each year at Connecticut College.

Pale winter sun streaming through stained-glass windows lights the sanctuary of Harkness Chapel, where an exuberant mummers' play is under way.

And then the pageant begins, with a procession of guards and the Agincourt hymn sung by the Connecticut College chamber choir to greet Father and Mother Solstice, who are richly garbed in ermine and velvet. Members of the court, who place wreaths of ivy on concertgoers' heads, follow them. The choir leads the audience in the fifteenth-century English carol, "Make We Joy."

Mysterious dancers with racks of antlers perform the Abbots Bromley Horn Dance, a remnant of an ancient pagan religious ceremony in England. In a nod to the Druids, the Yule log is presented, and Morris dancers kick up their heels.

The St. Nicholas Songsters, children in jesters' costumes, warble English carols and West Indian songs. There is a Spanish guitar performance, modern dance, clog dancers, sword dancers, bawdy moments, and religious ones. And finally the cast leads the audience out of the chapel, all dancing and singing "Lord of the Dance," to the melody of the Shaker song, "Simple Gifts." A bonfire burns outside.

At the center of it all is Derron Wood (Class of '88), who has directed Make We Joy for twenty years.

The intricacy and diversity of the performance is impressive, but it's even more astonishing when you learn that the performers rehearse together only once, the day before the show, when Wood weaves it into a pageant.

"That's the spirit of Make We Joy—you never know what's going to happen," Wood says. "I always say to the cast: Remember—we are here to spread joy. If you can make someone laugh, you may have kicked off the beginning of their season in a way that is just so special for them."

Make We Joy is held the first Sunday in December.

Harkness Chapel
Connecticut College, New London, CT 06320
(860) 439-2450; www.conncoll.edu

REFORMING CHRISTMAS

Say the name Harriet Beecher Stowe and most people think of her book, *Uncle Tom's Cabin*, and the influence she had on abolishing slavery. But Stowe's causes went well beyond that issue. Did you know that the way we celebrate Christmas today was shaped by Stowe and other reformers of her era?

So says Katherine Kane, executive director of the Harriet Beecher Stowe Center in Hartford. She says in early America, there were two kinds of Christmas. "There was a rowdy party kind of Christmas, which involved lots of drinking. In a kind of exaggerated trick-or-treat, if you were a prosperous person, you could expect less-prosperous people to show up at your door and ask for drink and goodies," she says. "If you didn't give them any, they might break a window or something, and that was sort of accepted. The other kind of Christmas was Puritan Christmas, which was no Christmas at all. It was not on the calendar; it was just another day. There were no festivities whatsoever."

Harriet Beecher Stowe, born in 1811, was the daughter of a fire-and-brimstone Calvinist minister who did not celebrate Christmas. But as the American middle class grew in the 1820s and 1830s, popular culture began to change. The Beecher-Stowe families

were among the earliest New Englanders to adopt some of the new customs of Christmas, like decorated evergreen trees. Abolitionists even used "giving trees" as a way to raise money for their cause at antislavery fairs.

A visit to her home at Nook Farm in later years shows that the family hung stockings, wrapped presents, shared holiday feasts including oysters and other delicacies, and decorated Christmas trees.

But these social reformers also saw Christmas as an opportunity to practice charity, creating gift baskets for the poor and focusing on children.

Harriet Beecher Stowe wrote about Christmas many times. "In the 1850s she wrote a story called 'Christmas; Or the Good Fairy,' in which a woman was complaining there was too much shopping, it was too expensive, and there were too many things to do," says Katherine. "This all sounds very familiar to us. The solution Stowe suggests is that you should give those gifts to people who don't have as much as you do."

HARRIET BEECHER STOWE CENTER
77 Forest Street, Hartford, CT 06105
(860) 522-9258; www.harrietbeecherstowecenter.org

HILL-STEAD HOLIDAY

With its collection of paintings by Monet, Manet, and Degas, the Farmington home known as Hill-Stead hardly needs ornamentation at the holidays. But its owner, Theodate Pope Riddle, loved to entertain, and at Christmas her gracious home was the scene of elegant gatherings.

A pioneer woman architect, Theodate designed the thirty-nine-room mansion, now a National Historic Landmark, in 1901 for her parents, Alfred and Ada Pope. When they passed away, Theodate moved in with her husband, John Wallace Riddle. "They had guests from all over the world," says curator Cynthia Cormier. "Well-known authors, politicians, and artists flocked here." Novelist Henry James once called Hill-Stead "an exquisite palace of peace, light, and harmony." Sinclair Lewis, Thornton Wilder, Mary Cassatt, and Eleanor Roosevelt were among the guests, and you can be too. Early in December the staff re-creates the holidays at Hill-Stead, dressing in costume and portraying members of the Pope and Riddle families as they prepare for an evening of entertaining.

Theodate's sparkly frock is laid out on her bed. An antique Santa costume is spread on the chaise, in case Mr. Riddle chooses to portray Saint Nick for his guests. The butler greets you in the library,

where a Whistler painting hangs over the fireplace and white poinsettias are banked on the hearth. The dining room is set for a Christmas feast, with crystal and silver gleaming on the table.

When Theodate Pope Riddle died in 1946, she left Hill-Stead as a museum. According to her instructions, it is maintained today almost precisely the way it was when Theodate lived here.

HILL-STEAD MUSEUM
35 Mountain Road, Farmington, CT 06032
(860) 677-4787; Fax: (860) 677-0174
www.hillstead.org

SLEIGH BELLS RING

Jingling sleigh bells, tolling church bells, and the peals of handbells are sounds that define Christmas. In the late 1800s the bell-making capital of the world was East Hampton, Connecticut. Historians say there were as many as thirty companies making bells there, and East Hampton was

dubbed Belltown USA. Companies like Starr, Hill, and Gong were well known.

Bevin Brothers was the second bell company established in East Hampton and is now the only company left in America that makes nothing but bells. William Bevin learned the art of bell making while working as an indentured servant, and when he went home to East Hampton, he and his brothers, Chauncey and Abner, started the Bevin Brothers bell factory in 1832. A fourth brother, Philo, later joined the others, and in 1868 Bevin Brothers was incorporated as the Bevin Brothers Manufacturing Company. The brothers made sleigh, hand-, cow-, sheep, door-, and ship's bells. They made more than twenty sizes of sleigh bells after a law was passed requiring them to be placed on sleighs to warn pedestrians and other traffic of their silent approach. Later the brothers made the first bicycle bells.

Bevin Brothers Manufacturing Company still makes dozens of varieties of bells in an old brick factory building. Six generations of Bevins have overseen operations, and Stanley Bevin says proudly, "We are the oldest family-owned manufacturing firm in the state." They were also one of the first companies in Connecticut to make toys, but today they just make bells. Think of a classic Currier & Ives scene of a horse-drawn sleigh gliding through the snow, and those might be Bevin bells jingling on the harnesses. Bevin Brothers makes nickel- or brass-plated decorative bells to hang on Christmas trees, brass handbells, copper cowbells, and lots of special orders with colorful commemorative lettering. Stanley says they've even outfitted Santa with bells for his reindeer. "We like to think that we've definitely contributed to the joy that Santa spreads."

Bevin Brothers Manufacturing Company
10 Bevin Road, East Hampton, CT 06424
(860) 267-4431; www.bevinbells.com

Royal Tea Scones

2½ cups all-purpose flour
1 tablespoon baking powder
½ teaspoon salt
1 stick of unsalted butter, cold
¼ cup granulated sugar
⅔ cup milk
A handful of currants

Makes about twelve scones.

1. Heat the oven to 425 degrees Fahrenheit. Line a baking sheet with parchment paper. In a mixer bowl, add flour, baking powder, salt, sugar, and currants. Mix to blend.
2. Mix in the butter, cut up into little pieces. Add milk. Blend until a soft dough forms. Form into a ball and place on a lightly floured board. Give ten to twelve kneads.
3. Roll out dough and cut scones with round cutter, until all the dough has been used. Bake for about twelve minutes, or until golden on top.

A ROYAL CUP OF TEA

At this hectic season of the year, how about slowing down for a soothing cup of tea? Even better, how about a properly served English tea, complete with tea cakes, tea sandwiches, and scones topped with clotted cream and jam? Those are some of the delights Carol Timpanelli's Royal Tea Company serves at the teas she caters year-round, and some special ones she does every year at the holidays. One of her biggest is the tea for 250 guests that's become part of the tradition at the Fairfield Christmas Tree Festival. One of her favorites is a tea for about eighty people served at her friend Barbara Bellinger's Tudor home in Bridgeport.

When Barbara moved into the house, she remembers thinking, "This is a winter house. This is a Christmas house." So every year Barbara erects a twelve-foot tree to hold court in the living room. A balcony is the perfect place for a chamber group to play, and the strains of Christmas carols greet the guests as they arrive for Barbara's annual Christmas tea.

In the dining room silver epergnes hold long stems of crimson roses, or a fat green pear. Red satin ribbons dangle from the brass chandelier. There are tea sandwiches stuffed with almond chicken, watercress, and cucumber, and chocolate toffee trifle served by young women in lace-trimmed pinafores over candy-cane-striped skirts. Darjeeling tea is steeping in a china teapot.

Carol started the Royal Tea Company twenty years ago, when a paralyzing illness left her unable to walk for months. On an earlier trip to London she had enjoyed an elegant tea and thought, *There is a niche for this in Connecticut, if it's done beautifully and elegantly.* While she recovered, Carol lay on her sofa reading books about British teas and dreaming about opening her own company. Since then her customers have included Martha Stewart and the Duchess of York.

One of her signature sweets is a star-shaped shortbread cookie, threaded with a fine satin ribbon. "You eat the cookie and then tie the ribbon around your finger; make a wish, and it's guaranteed to come true," says Carol.

ROYAL TEA COMPANY
5628 Main Street, Trumbull, CT 06611-3029
(203) 452-1006; www.royalteacompany.net

CHRISTMAS CLASSICS

The **New Haven Symphony Orchestra** gave their inaugural concert in January 1895, making it the fourth-oldest symphony orchestra to be formed in America, right behind the New York Philharmonic, the Boston Symphony, and the Chicago Symphony. The NHSO performs many of their concerts at historic Woolsey Hall at Yale but in recent years has made it their mission to serve a wider audience throughout Connecticut. During the holiday season the orchestra performs in halls along the shoreline and elsewhere, presenting classics like their version of the magnificent Handel's *Messiah*, as interpreted by music director William Boughton.

The music and the setting are perfect at **Orchestra New England**'s Colonial Concert, a holiday tradition for nearly thirty years. Attired in eighteenth-century finery, the orchestra performs in one of New Haven's historic churches on the green. The United Church of Christ congregation was formed in 1742 when members separated from the established church in New Haven. Not long after, Joseph Haydn wrote his magnificent "Oxford Symphony," *Symphony No. 92*, which Orchestra New England now performs in its annual "Concert of Muſick." This is a concert the Founding Fathers

of our nation might have enjoyed—and in a setting where they would feel at home. The church is festooned for Christmas and lighted by candles. With a strong tradition of fine music, the United Church of Christ is home to a pipe organ, three grand pianos, and an Italian harpsichord. Conductor and orchestra founder Jim Sinclair plays his part, costumed and coiffed in a powdered wig. Following the concert, mulled wine is served in the church hall, completing the atmosphere of a Colonial soiree.

Other holiday performing groups include the **Hartford Chorale,** a symphonic chorus more than

150 voices strong, which often performs *Messiah* or other masterworks at Christmas. The **Connecticut Master Chorale** performs in the Danbury area. The holiday concerts are accompanied by a brass and percussion ensemble. This group has performed at Carnegie Hall, Lincoln Center, and West Point Military Academy. The **Waterbury Chorale** is composed of singers from nearly thirty communities in Connecticut. Their holiday repertoire includes J. S. Bach's *Christmas Oratorio* and Benjamin Britten's *A Ceremony of Carols* and *St. Nicholas Cantata*.

New Haven Symphony Orchestra
P.O. Box 9718, New Haven, CT 06536
(203) 865-0831, ext. 10
www.newhavensymphony.org

Orchestra New England
P.O. Box 200123, New Haven, CT 06520-0123
(203) 777-4690; www.orchestranewengland.org

www.hartfordchorale.org

www.cmchorale.org

www.waterburychorale.org

CHRISTMAS CITY OF CONNECTICUT

"Never have we seen such brilliant and effective city and home decorations in any city. That this should prevail so soon after Norwich was devastated by flood and hurricane is an amazing example of the courage of the people." That's what the judges of holiday decorations in Norwich said in 1938, after declaring the winners of the city's home-decorating contest. It's that spirit that made Norwich the Christmas City of Connecticut, a title it captured several times in the years leading up to World War II in a competition that included as many as eight other cities. Norwich is still proud of that designation and determined to keep that spirit alive. After all, the city has survived for 350 years.

Kathy Relyea had heard tales of how the city outdid itself in holiday displays in the 1920s and 1930s, and how the "canopy of lights" over Franklin Square and the light-bedecked gingerbread of Norwich City Hall attracted shoppers and tourists. In the late 1980s she kicked off a campaign to light up city hall once again. And although Norwich is no longer a shopping mecca, the city twinkles and glows each winter, thanks to Kathy—fondly known as the Christmas Lady of Norwich.

The annual lighting of city hall the day after Thanksgiving signals the start of the Norwich Winter Festival, which stretches almost until Christmas Day, and includes art shows, the sale of a specially designed commemorative ornament, a storefront-decorating contest, and the city-wide house-decorating contest. The highlight is the Norwich Winter Festival parade, which lasts nearly two hours and takes place the afternoon of the second Sunday after Thanksgiving. The parade features more than twenty floats, costumed characters from history, decorated fire engines, horse-drawn carriages, marching bands, Scouts, Shriners, and, of course, the arrival of Santa Claus.

www.norwichct.org

SNOW QUEEN

A brace of blond Belgian draft horses clip-clops down the long tree-lined driveway, as Santa and Mrs. Claus and elf Mary make their grand entrance in a horse-drawn wagon for an appearance at the White Memorial Conservation Center. This environmental education center and nature museum is located in the heart of the four-thousand-acre White Memorial Foundation in the hills of northwestern Connecticut.

Fred Bunnell and his horses deliver their passengers to Santa's cottage, where children wait their turn for a few minutes on Santa's lap, to tell him of their hopes for Christmas morning. Santa's "cottage," a classroom in the education center, is

decorated with a Victorian-style tree and antique taxidermy.

Outside the cottage, the center's forest superintendent, Lukas Hyder, stokes a bonfire where guests can warm up and sing a carol or two with Mrs. Claus and her elf friend, Mary.

Fred and his team of horses shuttle families to the Carriage House, where a puppet show is about to take place. The Carriage House is decked out with a huge fir tree cut on the property, festooned with hundreds of white lights and candy canes. Tables overflowing with sugary treats beckon families, while bottomless cups of velvety hot chocolate, made from scratch and topped with whipped cream, pour out of the kitchen.

The audience settles in for a presentation of the Hans Christian Andersen classic "The Snow Queen," performed by Robin McCahill. The Thomaston artist is known for her felted scarves, sweaters, and hats. She also creates puppet and marionette shows, some original and some adaptations of classic fairy tales. Robin voices all of the characters and creates each of the hand-felted puppets in her whimsical troupe. "The Snow Queen" is a tale of friends lost and found, visits to distant lands, travels through changing seasons, and encounters with strange and exotic characters. "I love the story because the hero is a girl, and that's a positive message that many fairy tales don't have. The themes are about choosing good over bad, and following your heart."

Admission to the event is a nonperishable food item, to be donated by the Harwinton Girl Scouts to a local food pantry. If there is snow, bring your cross-country skis or snowshoes and explore the White Memorial Foundation's thirty-five miles of trails.

White Memorial Conservation Center, Inc.
80 Whitehall Road, P.O. Box 368
Litchfield, CT 06759
(860) 567-0857; www.whitememorialcc.org

For more about Robin McCahill, visit:
www.intuit2arts.com

ALL DECKED OUT

Across the street from the New Britain Museum of American Art, there is a holiday exhibit that rivals any in Connecticut, at the home of Rita Giancola.

Dozens of lighted characters line the lawn and rooftop, and carols resound from outside speakers. Inside, it's a sparkling Christmas fantasyland in every room. Eighty-five-year-old Rita spends two months setting up the decorations with some help from her sixteen grandchildren and eight great-grandchildren. But, she says, "I do 95 percent of it myself."

I asked Rita whether she knows of anyone else who has ever put together such an elaborate display. "Not to my knowledge, and no one ever will," she says. Her daughter Debi agrees. "This is the best homemade holiday house in the U.S., inside and outside!" says Debi. "People get so much joy here. Last night one couple came in and they started waltzing in the living room."

Rita has collected thousands of decorations for decades. An army of animated figures inhabits the rooms, along with a huge tree and miles of garland and lights. The dining-room table is set with Christmas china, cutlery, and crystal.

To some, it might look a little overdone. But not to Rita. "Oh, no. I see some spaces I have to fill." The only one I see is the kitchen sink. From chandeliers to shower curtains, it seems that every square inch is decorated for the holidays.

Visiting the house is a tradition for hundreds of people each year. It started in 1978, when Rita noticed passersby peeking into her windows. So she started holding an open house for a few evenings the week before Christmas. The admission charge is the donation of a nonperishable food item for a needy family.

And that, says Rita, is the true meaning of Christmas. "It means giving. We all do too much taking and not enough giving." In her festive way, Rita Giancola gives Christmas back its real meaning.

RITA GIANCOLA
61 Lexington Street, New Britain, CT 06052-1412

AHEAD OF HER TIME

Frances Osborne Kellogg was a woman ahead of her time. When her father died in 1907, she took over the family businesses, which had been started by her grandfather, one of Naugatuck Valley's early industrial entrepreneurs. Within a year, they were all more profitable than they had been.

"She did find it difficult in the beginning to conduct business, being the sole businesswoman in the valley," says Will Stoddard, former director of the Osborne Homestead Museum in Derby. "She succeeded because of her determination."

Fanny often invited friends to Osbornedale, her home and estate, for lectures and performances by some of the most interesting people of the day. Her home is now a museum.

When Fanny married Waldo Stewart Kellogg, he became interested in the family dairy herd and bred Holsteins. In 1956 the dairy farm and estate were given to the people of Connecticut by Frances Osborne Kellogg.

The dairy farm, adjacent to the house, is now the four-hundred-acre Osbornedale State Park and the site of the Kellogg Environmental Center. In winter its rolling hills and meadows attract snowshoers and cross-country skiers. There's ice-skating on Pickett's Pond and a pavilion for warming up. Guided bird walks are offered throughout the season.

The Colonial Revival house itself is especially beautiful at the holidays. Five Naugatuck Valley garden clubs decorate it with floral arrangements and holiday displays that complement Fanny's European antiques, her porcelain collection, and the gleaming silver pieces made by one of her own companies. There are guided tours, including one by candlelight.

In the living room, Fanny's rare leather-bound and gilt-trimmed third edition of *A Christmas Carol* by Charles Dickens is placed on a table, and the holiday decorations reflect the time she lived there.

After touring the home, you may want to attend a workshop at the Kellogg Environmental Center.

One of the most accomplished women of her day, Frances Osborne Kellogg left a precious legacy for all when she willed her home, her farm, and her holiday hospitality to the people of Connecticut.

OSBORNEDALE STATE PARK
555 Roosevelt Drive, Derby, CT 06418
(203) 735-4311; www.ct.gov/dep

MARCHING TO A HOLIDAY BEAT

Holiday spirit is on the march in Connecticut in a tradition that goes back to Colonial times: a wintertime parade. According to local historians, in early America the local militia would march to the village green with their fifes and drums in early December. When the townspeople heard the music, they would rush from their homes, carrying torches and lanterns. Old Saybrook revived the tradition more than thirty years ago, and the **Christmas Torchlight Parade and Muster** attracts about forty Ancient Fife and Drum Corps. Spectators carry torches, lanterns, and flashlights. As the last parade unit passes, the crowd falls in behind them for the Community Carol Sing.

Two surfers from California who moved to Connecticut came up with one of the most popular holiday events in southeastern Connecticut. The **East Lyme Light Parade** steps off down Main Street just after dark on the second Sunday in December. Every entry in the parade is lighted, whether it's an elaborate float resembling a carousel, marching Brownies sporting strands of battery-operated lights, or musicians in the marching band, lighting their instruments. Twelve thousand people have been known to show up, and many bring nonperishable food items to load onto a special food-drive float.

The **Groton White Lights Holiday Parade** follows the "Miracle Mile" through the business district. At the end of the parade, Santa lights the community tree, and everyone joins in a carol sing. More than sixty marching units and floats compete for trophies, and Santa lights the tree after the parade. The Groton Business Association (GBA) of the Greater Mystic Chamber of Commerce holds the Groton parade on the first Saturday of December at 5:00 p.m.

The **Montville Holiday Light Parade** is a relative newcomer, but residents say the event is growing. Most of the marchers are Scouts, though the fire department has come up with some imaginative entries, including a fire truck done up to look like a house on fire. The parade heads down Route 32 through town at dusk on the first Sunday in December.

In Stamford the holiday season steps off the Sunday before Thanksgiving with the **UBS Parade Spectacular,** featuring twenty-five helium balloons, thirteen marching bands, floats, and dance troupes. The parade draws over one hundred thousand spectators, and more than one thousand volunteers, like balloon handler Sonya Van Norden and her team from the Boys and Girls Club of Stamford. The fun starts Saturday afternoon when families flock to the "balloon blowup" on Hoyt Street. When inflated, the helium balloons are as tall as nearby office buildings.

Spectator Carolyn Ligi says, "We have our own tradition. We don't have to go to New York to see a big parade!"

CHRISTMAS TORCHLIGHT PARADE AND MUSTER
www.oldsaybrookct.org

EAST LYME LIGHT PARADE
www.discovereastlyme.com

GROTON WHITE LIGHTS HOLIDAY PARADE
www.grotonbiz.com

MONTVILLE HOLIDAY LIGHT PARADE
Montville Police Department: (860) 848-7510
or (860) 848-6500
Montville Parks and Recreation Department:
(860) 848-0277

UBS PARADE SPECTACULAR
www.stamford-downtown.com

HOLIDAY HOUSE TOURS

Many of us hold open houses for friends and family at this time of year, but imagine inviting several thousand people to traipse through your house to see your holiday decorations!

For more than forty years, the **Newcomers Club of New Canaan**'s Holiday House Tour has raised hundreds of thousands of dollars for local charities. The tour features five extraordinary homes of varying architectural styles, each decorated by professionals in unique holiday themes. One year, a celebrated Mid-Century Modern—designed and built by John Johansen, the last surviving member of the Harvard Five—was on the tour. Villa Ponte, which straddles the Rippowam River, has been featured in dozens of architectural publications. White and silver decorations set the tone for a 1960s New Year's Eve bash. In contrast, a dramatic country estate was also on the tour, decorated with candelabras, silver goblets, and garlands embellished with feathers, pinecones, and pomegranates. The home belongs to a television producer and British music exec, and their decorator included guitars signed by music greats like B. B. King.

The Friends of the **Mark Twain House** have opened some of greater Hartford's most intriguing homes to visitors at the holidays. The highlight of the tour (and its beneficiary) is the house where Mark Twain (Samuel Clemens) and his family lived from 1874 to 1891. This nineteen-room mansion is where Twain penned such classics as *The Adventures of Tom Sawyer*, *The Adventures of Huckleberry Finn*, and *A Connecticut Yankee in King Arthur's Court*. Louis Comfort Tiffany's design firm decorated the first floor of the house. Clemens described the house as having "a heart and a soul." At Christmastime the house is decorated as though Clemens family members might step through the door.

Not only do house tours give you a chance to peek inside homes you've probably passed by and wondered about, but they're also great for decorating ideas. Local florists and decorators often let their imaginations run free as they create holiday displays that complement the unique qualities of the homes. That's what you'll find on the **Westport Historical Society** holiday tour, which opens some of the grandest homes on the "Gold Coast."

www.newcanaannewcomers.com/hht

www.marktwainhouse.org

www.westporthistory.org

A FINE FEATHERED CHRISTMAS

The Audubon Society calls it "the longest-running Citizen Science survey in the world." For 110 years, from Alaska to Antarctica, tens of thousands of volunteers participate in the annual Christmas Bird Count.

In earlier times the Christmas Side Hunt was a common holiday practice. Hunters assigned to teams went out with their guns; whichever team brought back the most birds and other game won. But on Christmas Day 1900, Frank Chapman, a member of the newly formed Audubon Society, began a new tradition that has taken its place. Chapman's idea was not to kill birds but to count them. Both the conservation movement and the Christmas Bird Count have taken off since then.

Connecticut was part of that first count, and bird lovers in Connecticut continue to count our feathered friends to this day. In 1900 twenty-seven people in all counted birds in twenty-five areas, or "count circles" (the specific geographical areas designated by the Audubon Society). About 18,500 individual birds were counted, mostly in the northeastern part of North America.

Now, 110 years later, more than forty-five thousand Americans in nearly nineteen hundred circles count more than fifty-four million individual birds! It's not uncommon for birders in Connecticut to record one hundred species inland during the Christmas Bird Count, and more on the shoreline. A record number of wild turkeys was recorded in the Hartford area, and birders found two snowy owls, something of a rarity in the state.

Anyone can participate in the CBC, which takes place between December 14 and January 5 each year. A count compiler, who is an experienced birdwatcher, leads each circle. If you live within a count circle, you can stay home and report the birds that visit your feeder, or join a group of birdwatchers in the field.

www.audubon.org

CHRISTMAS WITH THE GOVERNOR

As Governor M. Jodi Rell stands poised in the front entry of her home, dressed in a holiday sweater and slacks, she looks like anyone else greeting guests for a holiday open house. But at this open house there won't be just a few dozen people; there will be a few thousand. And although most of them have never met the eighty-seventh governor of Connecticut, many will call her by her first name, Jodi. That's the friendly and warm atmosphere this governor has established at the official residence on Prospect Avenue in Hartford.

"This house truly belongs to the public," Governor Rell says. "This gives families from across the state the opportunity to see the Governor's Residence decorated for the holidays." And it is beautifully decorated, by the florists, landscapers, and greenhouse growers of Connecticut who scurry through the residence the day before it opens to the public, decorating trees, dressing mantelpieces, and setting an elegant dining-room table.

First Lady Claudia Weicker started the tradition in 1992. The house had been neglected for years before the Weickers moved in. The night that plaster fell onto visiting dignitaries in the dining room, Mrs. Weicker found support for a renovation campaign, which has been paid for with private donations.

In the foyer, Connecticut-grown poinsettias bank the grand staircase. In the front parlor, the parquetry floor incorporates the state seal with its Latin motto, *Sustinet qui transtulit* ("He who transplanted sustains").

The dining room is elegant, with wall coverings of silk damask and dried amaranths hanging from the fireplace mantel like cranberry-colored icicles. The sunroom is warmed by yellow paint and wicker furniture.

The Rells are the thirteenth family to live in the governor's official residence, which was purchased in 1943. The three-story brick and limestone Georgian Revival–style home has nineteen rooms, nine fireplaces, a greenhouse, a pergola, and a reflecting pool, and is set on six acres at 990 Prospect Avenue, at the corner of Asylum Avenue.

Holiday Open House Tour
990 Prospect Avenue, Hartford, CT 06105
Begins the Wednesday after Thanksgiving.
Admission is one new, unwrapped toy to be given to a needy child.

HOLLY JOLLY TROLLEY

Frank Rossano is wearing a red Rudolph nose and a lighted hat shaped like a puffy Christmas tree with his formal motorman's uniform. On a chilly December night after a fresh snow, Frank is pulling Car 4 out of the trolley barn for the evening's festivities at **The Connecticut Trolley Museum**'s Winterfest.

Car 4 is painted gold, and is wide open with amphitheater seating for the best views. "Car 4 is our most popular car because the windows are so crystal clear, and we never to have to wash them," Frank jokes. Heavily bundled-up families pile into the car once known as "the Golden Chariot" when it was used for sightseeing in Montreal in the 1920s.

Whistles blow and brass bells ring as antique streetcars take you on a three-mile trip through the countryside of East Windsor. The trolley takes you through a tunnel of lights, in an area decorated just for Christmas.

After your trolley ride, don't miss the spectacular exhibit inside the visitor center, where George Contrada and his fellow model-train buffs have nine complete setups, with multiple trains running on each. There is even a train within a trolley, as an antique trolley car becomes a platform for an elaborate train setup. There are five other trolley cars decked out with lights and trees and all manner of ornaments.

Winterfest runs on selected evenings in November and December, starting just after Thanksgiving.

In East Haven **The Shore Line Trolley Museum** runs the Branford Electric Railway, said to be the oldest continuously operating suburban trolley line in the United States. On weekends after Thanksgiving, you can ride a cozy heated trolley and visit with Santa, complete with cookies, hot chocolate, a Lionel train exhibit, and a gift for the kids. The museum recently started an illuminated nighttime trolley ride for one evening just before Christmas.

THE CONNECTICUT TROLLEY MUSEUM
58 North Road, East Windsor, CT 06088
(860) 627-6540; www.cttrolley.org

THE SHORE LINE TROLLEY MUSEUM
17 River Street, East Haven, CT 06512
(203) 467-6927; www.bera.org

NUTCRACKERS

The Nutcracker may be the most familiar and beloved ballet in the world. With music by Tchaikovsky and a dreamlike story of a young girl and her nutcracker prince, the traditional version has entertained families during the holidays for more than a hundred years. But Connecticut has a tradition of unconventional *Nutcracker*s.

American Nutcracker garnered national attention when it debuted. The Hartford Ballet set the tale in the American Southwest during the gold rush of the 1800s. *American Nutcracker* featured traditional sugarplum fairies and snowflakes, but there were also honeybees, a giant spider, and a golden eagle too. Sunflowers danced with butterflies.

The Hartt School's version was *Nutcracker in a Nutshell*, a one-hour version of *The Nutcracker* choreographed by Adam Miller, who included a dash of the Marx Brothers and the Three Stooges. The sword scenes, he said, "come from memories of my own living-room battles with my brothers." He set the tale in a sea captain's home in Connecticut.

Perhaps the most unusual version is the new interpretation presented by Goran and Desiree Subotic. Their advertising for *A Mystic NUT! Cracker* warns: "You may not be ready for this!" Their ballet, staged in the Pequot Auditorium at the Mashantucket Pequot Museum at Foxwoods, attracts families with little girls in twirly dresses and beribboned ponytails, as well as audiences looking for a new twist on a classic. "It's fresh. It's new. It's provocative," says Goran, the founder of **Mystic Ballet.** "It's food for people who want to experience something different."

The troupe features dancers from as near as Massachusetts and as far away as Mongolia. The basic elements of the story are included, but the production is set in contemporary times. Instead of finding her prince in her dreams, Clara finds him on Facebook. Adults are intrigued by the reflections of Clara's parents on their marriage, and children

MYSTIC BALLET
325 Mistuxet Avenue, Stonington, CT 06378
(860) 536-3671; www.mysticballet.org

THE NUTMEG CONSERVATORY FOR THE ARTS
58 Main Street, Torrington, CT 06790
(860) 482-4413; www.nutmegconservatory.org

CONNECTICUT BALLET
20 Acosta Street, Stamford, CT 06902
(203) 964-1211
Hartford Office
99 Pratt Street, Suite 209, Hartford, CT 06103
(860) 293-1039; www.connecticutballet.com

laugh out loud when dancing Santas leap across the stage or gather in the Lotus position for a meditation session. While presenting the classic score, there's also a little bit of Guy Lombardo and Bing Crosby seasonal music thrown in for good measure.

For a more traditional *Nutcracker,* one of my favorites is **The Nutmeg Conservatory**'s production presented in Hartford and in Torrington, where the students complete their high school training and begin their professional training.

The **Connecticut Ballet** based in Stamford is the state's professional ballet company, contracting seasonally with dancers from well-known companies like the American Ballet Theatre and the Alvin Ailey American Dance Theater. Artistic director Brett Raphael's production of *The Nutcracker* is lush.

UNSILENT NIGHT

A boom-box symphony with a procession is one way to describe composer Phil Kline's *Unsilent Night*. Others have called it ethereal, euphoric, and avant-garde. The processional starts at the Yale Bookstore in New Haven and winds its way through town to the giant Christmas tree on the green along a pathway lighted with luminaria. The marchers are also the musicians. Each participant carries a boom box or a music player with speakers that will play a CD or MP3. Each one plays one of four musical parts. The combination fills the air with the sounds of bells and otherworldly voices—what composer Phil Kline calls "electronic caroling."

Unsilent Night debuted on the sidewalks of Greenwich Village in 1992 and is now a holiday tradition worldwide, from San Francisco to Sydney. "*Unsilent Night* is an outdoor, ambient music piece," Kline says. "It's like a Christmas-caroling party except that we don't sing, but rather carry the music, each of us playing a separate track that is a 'voice' in the piece. When I created it, I was hoping to show that sometimes good things do come right out of thin air."

The International Festival of Arts and Ideas brings many fresh performances and artists to the city each June, but this has become their holiday-season tradition. Mary Lou Aleskie, the executive director of the Festival, calls Kline "an innovative musician, who is as comfortable in the rock world as he is in the conservatory." Recently he was invited to collaborate with choreographer Wally Cardona and the New Haven community to create "Really Real," a dance/music performance that premiered at the International Festival of Arts & Ideas.

The *New York Times* calls *Unsilent Night* "a swirling blizzard of sound," but the people who play in the boom-box symphony in New Haven simply call it a lot of fun. People of all ages can participate—no experience necessary!

FESTIVAL'S HOLIDAY HOTLINE
(203) 498-3727
E-mail: unsilentnight@artidea.org
www.unsilentnight.com

COME TO THE MANGER

In Bethlehem, once in the middle of the night and seven times throughout the day, a bell summons the nuns at the Abbey of Regina Laudis to chapel. In Latin they sing the Divine Office as handed down by Saint Benedict 1,400 years ago.  They are believed to be the only community of women in the United States pledged to preserve the ancient Gregorian chant. They do it, according to Mother Margaret Georgina, because "we were asked by Pope Paul VI to keep the Latin. He said the church has her language and someone has to keep it living."

The forty women live a contemplative life behind walls and enclosures, cloistered, for the most part, from the rest of the world. In their Church of Jesu Fili Mariae, as Catholics gather for morning mass, an evergreen stands before the altar, decorated with hundred of stars. A mobile with a star hangs above the tree. It was created by Mother Praxedes, who explains, "The star is leading us to Bethlehem and to the altar."

After three years of restoration, their magnificent crèche is once again on display in an eighteenth-century stable on the property. Sister Angele says, "We believe it was given to Victor Amadeus, the king of Sardinia, to mark his coronation in 1720." The crèche contains sixty-eight figures made of carved wood, terra-cotta, and porcelain. They are dressed in their original costumes and set in a village made from cork bark.

"What's fabulous about it," points out Sister Angele, "is the scene contains all manner of members of the village, so some of them are intensely focused on the baby Jesus and holy family while others are more involved with each other and village pursuits." What that means, she says, is that "everyone who comes to the crèche can find somebody that they relate to amidst all of these people."

The sisters sell trees and wreaths at Christmastime, and their shop is open year-round, offering pottery, ironwork, leather goods, artisanal cheeses, and more, all made at the abbey. CDs of the chant as sung by the sisters of the Abbey of Regina Laudis are the perfect soundtrack for contemplating the true meaning of Christmas.

ABBEY OF REGINA LAUDIS
273 Flanders Road, Bethlehem, CT 06751-2210
(203) 266-7727; www.abbeyofreginalaudis.com

A CONNECTICUT CHRISTMAS CAROL

A *Christmas Carol* was a tradition for Michael Wilson when he was growing up in North Carolina. Whether it was the movie version, which played at the local theater year after year, or the annual production of the Dickens classic by the North Carolina Shakespeare Festival, *A Christmas Carol* was an essential part of the holiday.

"They define a classic as being a great story and a timeless tale for the ages," says Michael, "and I think that this is certainly one of them."

As artistic director of the Hartford Stage, Wilson has made the stage production of *A Christmas Carol: A Ghost Story of Christmas* one of Connecticut's most popular Yuletide traditions. Since 1998 more than a quarter of a million people have seen the show at the Tony Award–winning theater. Wilson's version is spooky and magical, with Ebenezer Scrooge's ghosts flying about the theater, in a London setting that mixes elements of *Mary Poppins* and *The Wizard of Oz*.

The story of a miser's Christmas Eve adventure and how it changes his life is a theme that brings people back every year, according to its longtime star, Bill Raymond, who plays Scrooge. "I think

this play makes a difference," Bill says. "People reconnect with its theme."

They certainly connect with Raymond and the rest of the cast, who get standing ovations at every performance. Raymond says some people have come back every year, and that they laugh "before I tell the jokes."

Wilson's adaptation of the story takes almost all the dialogue directly from Charles Dickens's novella. He plays up the ghost story with its phantasmagorical elements, but even the youngest children can enjoy one special family-friendly performance where they get to meet the ghostly apparitions beforehand.

Wilson likes to think that his audience goes on an emotional journey with Scrooge that makes them realize "how precious each moment of life is. I think you hear the story anew each year; you hear different things based on how you lived that last year. I certainly hear it differently at forty-five than I did at age six."

HARTFORD STAGE
50 Church Street, Hartford, CT 06103
(860) 527-5151; www.hartfordstage.org

DASHING THROUGH THE SNOW

Like the old Hank Snow song, 'I've been everywhere, man, I've been everywhere,' I've traveled through every one of the lower forty-eight United States many, many times," says Terry Joseph. Terry figures that during his years as a long-haul truck driver, he has racked up millions of

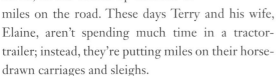

miles on the road. These days Terry and his wife, Elaine, aren't spending much time in a tractor-trailer; instead, they're putting miles on their horse-drawn carriages and sleighs.

"As soon as we get an inch or two of snow we start getting calls about sleigh rides," says Elaine, "but really, you need more like five or six inches." But when the white stuff piles up, they love hitching up Duke or Diesel to the sleigh and dashing through the snow in their one-horse open sleigh. O'er the fields they go, from their Cedar Knoll Farm in Lisbon, Connecticut, to destinations like a nearby winery or just through woodlands and pastures.

The Josephs own one of the biggest carriage companies in the state, and you'll see them at special events all over, driving their pure white Cinderella carriage or an open vis-à-vis at weddings or in parades. They are always nattily turned out, and the horses, mostly Percherons or Percheron-Belgian crosses, are bathed and groomed and nearly as sparkly as their carriages and sleighs. They own seven draft horses, or about seven tons of horseflesh.

"To me there is nothing like a dappled gray Percheron," says Terry, who explains that the horses grow whiter as they mature. "They tend to be a little more refined than some of the other draft breeds," says Elaine, "and they are quick on their feet."

Terry and Elaine have both loved horses since they were kids, and Terry has worked as a cowboy on a cattle ranch, and has bought, sold, and trained horses. "These horses are part of our family," says Elaine. "They are animals we would never think of selling."

Gift certificates for carriage or sleigh rides make great Christmas gifts!

Cedar Knoll Farm, LLC
57 Kimball Road, Lisbon, CT 06351
(860) 376-8110; www.cedarknoll.net

Let's get comfy and nestled all snug in the train,
while visions of sugar plums dance in our brains.
As we steam through the night on the North Pole Express,
keep an eye out for Santa, a sight to impress.

—INVITATION FROM ESSEX STEAM TRAIN AND RIVERBOAT

NORTH POLE EXPRESS

Most of the year it is known as the **Essex Steam Train,** but when the holiday season rolls around, that train becomes the North Pole Express, a steam-powered sleigh taking families on a magical nighttime journey to the North Pole. Once the train ride is under way, each coach becomes a stage for a live musical performance of "The Night Before Christmas." Especially if there is a coating of snow to enhance the evening, this is one of the most enchanting field trips you can take with your children.

During the daytime in December, families can ride the Santa Special, powered by a steam engine that goes back to 1925. Passengers board at the old-fashioned train station, and then with a blast from the whistle, the train is on its way. Santa and Mrs. Claus burst into one of the train's antique railroad cars and children shriek with happiness.

Bob and Lisa Teixeira of Mystic are riding the train with their seven-year-old daughter, Amy, and three-year-old son, Luke. "We wanted Luke to experience this while he was young. Little boys seem to have a special liking for trains," says Bob.

Vintage decorations adorn the cars, and Christmas carols play throughout the one-hour trip from Essex to Chester and back. Railroad buffs will appreciate the authenticity of the restored parlor cars, but anyone will enjoy leaving today behind and riding off into a winter wonderland in one of the prettiest parts of Connecticut aboard the Essex Steam Train's Santa Special.

The **Railroad Museum of New England,** which operates the Naugatuck Railroad, runs scenic rides from its historic station in Thomaston to Torrington and Waterville. On weekends right after Thanksgiving through mid-December, vintage cars are decorated for the season and Christmas music plays on board. Santa and Mrs. Claus greet passengers as the train travels through some of the prettiest countryside in the valley. If it's a white Christmas, the railroad is prepared: It has its own vintage rail snowplow.

Essex Steam Train
1 Railroad Avenue, Essex, CT 06426-1516
(860) 767-0103; www.essexsteamtrain.com

Railroad Museum of New England
242 East Main Street, Thomaston, CT 06787
(860) 283-7245; www.rmne.org

EVERYTHING OLD IS NEW AGAIN

Charles Dickens's *A Christmas Carol* is a holiday staple, but in Connecticut, two new theatrical pieces centered on the season are making their marks.

Some people call the **HartBeat Ensemble**'s *Ebeneeza: A Hartford Holiday Carol* a "ghetto" Christmas Carol, and according to artistic director Julia Rosenblatt, "that's what it is. That is what it was in Dickens's time. It was, and is, the story of people living in bitter poverty within a world of abundant riches."

In HartBeat's version, Ebeneeza is a woman, and the intriguing element of crafting the play is that the words come from interviews with people who live in Hartford. The play evolves each season, based on events that happened in the city during the previous year. There are also references to Hartford history, like Mark Twain as the Ghost of Christmas Past who haunts Ebeneeza's dreams.

Ebeneeza is performed in a number of venues during the Christmas season, and several of the performances are free.

A Civil War Christmas: An American Musical Celebration is on its way to becoming a new holiday tradition in the Elm City. Written by Pulitzer Prize–winning playwright Paula Vogel, the show had its world premiere at Long Wharf Theater and has been presented by the **New Haven Theater Company,** a community ensemble. Vogel, who is the chair of the Playwriting Department at the Yale School of Drama, said about the play, "It came to me in this flash—four or five stories that all collided at Christmas, Lincoln's Christmas in 1864." A cast of thirty actors portray ninety characters, including President Lincoln and his wife, Mary Todd Lincoln; assassin John Wilkes Booth; an escaped slave; a soldier boy; and cameos by Robert E. Lee, Ulysses S. Grant, and Walt Whitman. The New Haven Theater Company performs in nontraditional settings, to try to connect with new audiences for theater.

HartBeat Ensemble
233 Pearl Street, Hartford, CT 06103
(860) 548-9144; www.hartbeatensemble.org

T. Paul Lowry, Creative Director
New Haven Theater Company
(203) 891-5686; www.newhaventheatercompany.com

SANTA'S FIRE TRUCK

It takes a special person, committed to the community, to be a volunteer firefighter, and the members of the Long Hill Fire Company in Trumbull go out of their way to show that at Christmastime. Besides helping to keep their town safe, they also brighten the season for needy and sick kids, bringing holiday cheer to families all over town.

It started a few years ago with a toy drive at the firehouse. A few hundred toys were collected, but Fire Lieutenant Jay Leos, who is also a police officer in town, thought they could do more. Although the splashy decorations on the firehouse helped attract attention, Leos had another thought: What if they decorated one of the trucks that didn't get much use?

"Maxi the Truck is a 'special call' truck with the department, and it pretty much stays in the bay when the other trucks go out," says Leos. But after decking the truck out with Christmas lights and a snow machine, Maxi got a special call: to deliver toys to kids in town, with Santa on board. "The first year when we put lights on it, I swear it was smiling," Leos recalls with a smile.

That may have been Leos's imagination, which he puts to good use around the fire station. Every year he and the crew come up with new ways to adorn Maxi. They've added twelve thousand lights, a glowing fireplace that crackles and spouts smoke from a chimney, reindeer, and two complete Christmas villages, set up in the compartment that usually contains tools. From Thanksgiving through New Year's Day, they make special deliveries to local families who drop off a toy for their own kids and pay $50 for the visit. They've delivered a puppy to one family, and good news to another that a grandchild was on the way. The donations support the fire department and send burned children to special camps in the summer. Most of those families also drop off a toy for needy kids, as do many other people in town, to the tune of 1,300 toys last year.

"To make a long story short," says Leos, "a bunch of volunteer firefighters felt that no child in this town or anywhere else should go without a toy for the holidays, and we did something about it."

Deliveries are only made within Trumbull.

Long Hill Fire District Station #3
4229 Madison Avenue, Trumbull, CT 06611
www.longhillfd.com

GINGERBREAD TREASURES AND TREATS

The "Guru of Gingerbread" is what some people call **Teresa Layman,** who has written two books about building gingerbread houses. But the Warren artist is venturing into a new medium. Teresa explains how this came about: "I went low-carb a few years ago and lost eighty pounds. I gave up making gingerbread houses because I was afraid I would nibble." But she missed it. She also wanted something more permanent, "after having made so many gingerbread houses over the years and then feeding them to the squirrels after a season, watching all your hard work get eaten." So she now works in a claylike material that looks like gingerbread and even smells like gingerbread, but lasts forever. Teresa's "gingerbread" houses are scale miniatures—one inch equals one foot—and the level of detail is astonishing.

Her first creation, "The Gingerbread Kitchen," is the building at the North Pole where the elves make all the gingerbread houses for Christmas. On the shelves are teeny gingerbread houses, only about one inch tall. This one is in a museum in Kentucky. Now Teresa is working on "Twinkle Toes, Fine Elf Shoes," a little elf's shoemaker workshop. Although they can take six months or more to complete, Teresa is already planning the next project, "The Snowflake Factory." Eventually she thinks she will create the entire North Pole scene in everlasting "gingerbread."

Step inside the church hall at **St. George's Episcopal Church** in Middlebury, and your nose will lead you to the room where an elaborate gingerbread village has sprung up.

Marilyn Terrell remembers the first such gingerbread village here more than thirty years ago. It fit on a card table. "Now it takes up a whole room," she says, leading us on a tour of a make-believe community with sixty-five buildings made from the pungent cookie dough, united by paths paved in poppy seed and lined with kidney-bean walkways.

"Everything is edible. That's the only rule," she explains. After that, the construction crew can let their imaginations run wild. Practically the entire parish is involved, and it's not unusual to find three generations in one family laboring over their creation.

The gingerbread village is on display for one week each year. Every house is for sale.

www.teresalayman.com

St. George's Episcopal Church
393 Tucker Hill Road, Middlebury, CT 06762-2430
(203) 758-9864
http://netministries.org/see/churches.exe/ch05269

SANTA'S WORKSHOP

Think of Fairfield County and most people think of the "Gold Coast," big houses and big incomes. But there are children there who wouldn't enjoy Christmas without a little love from strangers. At a pre-holiday gift-wrapping party in Stamford, a gymnasium rocks with pop holiday music as an assembly line of "elves" works hard to make sure Santa's sack is filled with toys for needy kids. You can almost touch the Christmas spirit in the air!

Volunteer Olivia Stella is a Girl Scout from Stamford, who says she loses count after wrapping ten or eleven gifts. She is imagining the reactions of the children who will open those packages on Christmas morning. "I think the kids' hearts are going to feel warmed when they open them," she says.

The four thousand gifts are the result of a toy drive that provides presents for two thousand children. The gym is packed with long tables, hundreds of volunteers, miles of gift wrap and ribbon, and plenty of tape and scissors.

Morgan Henry puts the finishing touches on Elmo, and then turns to a jewelry and makeup kit designed for a little girl. At another table stuffed animals and picture books are going into glittery bags tied with ribbon.

The toys will be distributed to kids whose lives are affected by poverty, homelessness, and AIDS. For some, these are the only gifts they'll receive.

Takeia McAlister is the holiday gift collection manager for St. Luke's LifeWorks. She walks briskly among the gift wrappers, wearing reindeer antlers and smiling. "The holiday spirit comes out the most when people are wrapping and giving," she says.

St. Luke's LifeWorks offers educational opportunities, coaching and mentoring, and transitional and supportive housing to families in need. Each year their toy drive and wrapping parties get bigger.

Kelly Copeland has been helping out for thirteen years, "Each year if we get one person that gets that 'feel-good feeling,' they will bring more and more people, so it's the domino effect."

The wrapping parties have gotten so big, they have to hold them in two shifts now, with over four hundred people showing up for each one. Manav Puri is a junior at Westhill High School in Stamford. "I want other kids to have something under the tree," he says. "So, why not give somebody a piece of what I have, because I am very lucky."

St. Luke's LifeWorks
141 Franklin Street, Stamford, CT 06901
(203) 388-0100; www.learnaliving.org

MAKING THE SEASON MEANINGFUL

For the past twenty years, on one night in December, the driveway of the **United Methodist Church** in Cheshire is transformed into the Road to Bethlehem. Congregation members set up ten scenes depicting the journey of Joseph and Mary, and populate each one with actors from the church. In the frigid night air they provide a drive-through religious experience for visitors. While getting into their costumes, they get a little coaching on holding their poses. "Now don't forget, angels, to hold your arms up . . . and if you're wearing headphones, make sure the wires are tucked inside your costumes." Reverend Stephen Volpe says that as visitors drive through, "They are really thinking about what this all means. It's powerful, and people tell us it makes the season more meaningful."

The **Valley Brook Community Church** in Granby presents its live nativity at Salmon Brook Park. Luminaria lead visitors to the manger scene inside a park band shell. Live animals, including a donkey, sheep, goats, and chickens from Simsbury's Fleming Farms, add a touch of reality to the tableau. Some visitors stop to kneel by the manger, despite the cold. "This is our gift to the community, which we're proud to be a part of," Pastor Clark Pfaff says.

In another corner of the state at the **Rowayton Elementary School Field,** Rowayton has all the charm of small-town Connecticut, but it's actually a section of one of Connecticut's larger cities, Norwalk. This waterfront "village" (as it considers itself) embraces community events, whether a summertime parade or the children's nativity pageant at Christmas. The nativity pageant dates back to the days following the assassination of President Kennedy in 1963. Rowayton resident Putsie Ritchey and her neighbors wanted to bring the community together and raise its spirits. They scrambled to assemble the nativity pageant and have held it ever since.

The program is ecumenical, with readings by a Catholic priest, a Methodist minister, and clergy from the United Church of Rowayton.

UNITED METHODIST CHURCH
205 Academy Road, Cheshire, CT 06410
(203) 272-4626; www.gbgm-umc.org/cheshireumc

VALLEY BROOK COMMUNITY CHURCH
10 Hartford Avenue, Granby, CT 06035
(860) 844-0001; www.valleybrookcommunity.org

ROWAYTON ELEMENTARY SCHOOL FIELD
www.rowaytonct.com/NativityPageant.html

CHRISTMAS BY LANTERN LIGHT

Christmas is a time for fantasy, and once you step into the re-created nineteenth-century village at Mystic Seaport, the magic begins. It is twilight and a costumed guide with a lantern leads a group of about twelve people into the world of Christmas Eve 1876. The hour-long progressive Lantern Light Tour, "Hope Amongst the Stars," takes visitors through the town of Greenmanville, where the Gardner family has struggled each Christmas since the War Between the States, when Captain Gardner was lost. For eleven years, the family has wondered what happened to him. Greenmanville's cobblestone streets are bustling with activity, as neighbors make their way through the village on foot and by horse-drawn omnibus. With only hurricane lamps to light the way, it is easy to be transported back in time.

The performance threads the story of the Gardner family through each stop along the guide's route, including several Greek Revival homes where trees are decorated with paper ornaments; the print shop; a ride on the omnibus; a walk aboard the *L. A. Dunton*, a 123-foot sailing schooner; and a stop at the tavern for a bit of cheer, music, and a traditional dance. There's time for a little fiddling by a lonely sailor at the Seamen's Friend Society hall, a nibble of a ginger cookie, and caroling outside the meetinghouse. Blended into the tour, participants learn a bit of local history about the time when Mystic was a busy coastal village and shipyard. Mingling with women in long skirts and bonnets and men in topcoats and fur hats, you might catch a glimpse of Kris Kringle in a hooded cape.

The plays are new each season, and families who have come once often return with friends the following season. That's why AAA has named Mystic, Connecticut, one of the Top Twelve Places in the Nation for Holiday Spirit, and *Time* magazine has named it one of the Top Ten Places to See at Christmas. Tours are offered on ten nights starting right after Thanksgiving, and it's best to order your tickets early. The gift and book shops are great places to find unusual holiday gifts with a nautical and maritime theme.

MYSTIC SEAPORT
75 Greenmanville Avenue, Mystic, CT 06355
(860) 572-5322; www.mysticseaport.org

SONGS OF JOY

"This is as close to hearing angels sing as we are likely to get in this life." That's what one music critic said about Chorus Angelicus. The Torrington-based children's choir brings together young singers from across Connecticut. Grammy-winning composer Paul Halley, a longtime performer with the Paul Winter Consort, founded it. The choir, and its adult component, Gaudeamus—the choral groups of **Joyful Noise, Inc.**—are now under the artistic direction of Nicholas White. Their Christmas Angelicus concerts feature original carols and arrangements by White, music by Halley, and songs of the season from different centuries and diverse composers. The music is interspersed with readings, and the Christmas Angelicus concert series is performed at five churches in Connecticut, chosen for their aesthetic and acoustic beauty. The choirs also have toured internationally.

Trinity Episcopal Church in New Haven dates back to 1752, when its organizers were able to buy a plot of land in a town of Congregationalists. The Trinity Choir of Men and Boys has been an institution in New Haven since its founding in 1885. Only six such choirs in the nation are older. The choral group carries on a tradition that began in the Middle Ages, but its newest twist is a girls' choir founded in 2003. The Boys Choir has given concerts at Carnegie Hall, Lincoln Center, the National Cathedral, and the Metropolitan Museum of Art, in addition to several European tours. The celebrated choral group has been a favorite at the White House, has worked with renowned conductor Robert Shaw, and has performed Leonard Bernstein's *Mass* with the composer in attendance. The choir's recordings include *Christmas around the World*, containing new and traditional music for Advent, Christmas, and Epiphany. Organist and choirmaster Walden Moore leads the choirs.

JOYFUL NOISE, INC.
P.O. Box 1051, Torrington, CT 06790
(860) 496-8841; www.chorusangelicus.org

The choirs are in residence at:
TRINITY EPISCOPAL CHURCH
220 Prospect Street, Torrington, CT 06790
(860) 482-6027; www.trinitytorrington.org

129 Church Street, New Haven, CT 06510
(203) 624-3101; www.trinitynewhaven.org

THREE KINGS DAY

On January 6, twelve days after Christmas, Latinos celebrate Three Kings Day. Known in other cultures as the Epiphany, "Dia de los Tres Reyes Magos" commemorates the biblical story of Wise Men Melchior, Caspar, and Balthazar, who followed the Star of Bethlehem to worship the newborn Christ child and to bring Him gifts of gold, frankincense, and myrrh. The night before Three Kings Day, Latino children traditionally leave hay in their shoes under their beds to feed the camels ridden by the kings. In the morning they find their shoes filled with gifts and treats.

In Hartford the holiday is celebrated with a parade down Park Street featuring finely costumed Magi riding proudly through the business district on ten-foot-tall camels and Paso Fino horses. Sometimes the kings are local dignitaries, like the fire chief or school superintendent. Salsa music sounds from open doorways. Crowds of kids gather on the street while older folks lean out of their apartment windows to watch the festivities.

The parade begins in front of the Spanish American Merchants Association and ends at the Pope Park Recreation Center, where children enjoy a party and presents—delivered by the kings!

In Bridgeport Hispanic firefighters portray the kings and deliver gifts to children. Ron Morales calls it an honor to dress in majestic robes and crowns to celebrate the Latino tradition. Kids get the day off from school, and Morales says that while they are happy to see the kings, shouts of joy break out when they spot the piles of toys.

In other cities with large Latino populations, like Norwich, New Haven, West Haven, and Danbury, the day may start with Mass in the local church and end with a feast that brings families together for a celebration. For some communities, Three Kings Day on January 6 is bigger than December 25.

TWELFTH NIGHT

The Boar's Head and Yule Log Festival celebrates the Epiphany, or twelfth day after Christmas. The most glorious and uplifting event of the Christmas season takes place in January at Hartford's Asylum Hill Congregational Church. The church built of Portland brownstone once claimed Mark Twain as a member. The soaring nave is beribboned and garlanded, and it seems a great medieval banquet is about to begin. A chamber group, jugglers, puppeteers, and strolling singers entertain. A magician performs, acrobats somersault up and down the aisles, and the audience chortles at a jester's tomfoolery with a dancing bear. Bagpipers enter the church, and the procession begins with a Highland dance.

Trumpets herald the entrance of the king and queen and their court as the choir sings, "The boar's head, as I understand, is the rarest dish in all this land."

The Boar's Head and Yule Log Festival is a spectacle with a cast, choir, and orchestra of 225 congregation members elaborately costumed and choreographed and accompanied by live animals. In medieval England the boar was a symbol of evil, and serving the boar's head at Christmas was symbolic of Christ's triumph over Satan. Boar's head festivals were popular at English manor houses in the seventeenth century. The custom was carried on in Colonial America—beginning in Connecticut, some say.

Lords and ladies are followed by a parade of cooks and staff, bearing squawking geese, doves cooing in cages, holly, and mistletoe. A punchbowl of steaming wassail is carried in, along with a giant mince pie and the boar's head borne on a pallet. Traditional English carols are sung, with the audience joining in.

Then the church is plunged into darkness, and a sprite arrives with woodsmen bearing the Yule log. Now the story of the nativity will be told, with Joseph and Mary arriving on a donkey. The Magi arrive bearing gold, frankincense, and myrrh, accompanied by a camel wearing a sequined saddlecloth. The audience "ooohs" as the beast bends to fit beneath the arched doorway.

A child carries a lighted candle into the darkened church, symbolizing the light of Christ coming into the world. The entire assembly kneels to

worship in prayer and joyous song. Finally, the Yule sprite returns, and the child and a monk carry the light forth into the world.

For pageantry and magnificent music, the Boar's Head Festival is king. It is also a moving portrayal of the reason for the season.

Asylum Hill Congregational Church
814 Asylum Avenue, Hartford, CT 06105
(860) 278-0785; www.ahcc.org

PHOTO SOURCES

ABOUT THE AUTHOR

Emmy Award–winning television journalist Diane Smith has been on the air in Connecticut since 1982. Her very popular series for Connecticut Public TV, *Positively Connecticut*, searches out the inspiring, warm, funny, and often downright strange stories that give Connecticut its character. For nine years Diane was co-host of the top-rated *Morning Show* on WTIC-AM News Talk 1080, with Ray Dunaway. Diane was also a news anchor and reporter for sixteen years at WTNH-TV in New Haven. In 2010 Diane was honored with the Governor's Award for Culture and Tourism for her long time efforts to promote Connecticut as a great place to live and visit.